# PROFIT
## FROM CHANGE

Retooling Your Agency for Maximum Profits

TROY KORSGADEN

# Profit from Change
## Retooling Your Agency for Maximum Profits

Copyright © 2005 by Troy L. Korsgaden

Editorial services for this book provided by Laura Belgrave, editorial consultant for publishing professionals.

Design and production by Jim Pietras & Asssociates.

For information or bulk purchase, please contact:

**Troy Korsgaden**
**Troy Korsgaden Systems**
**Central Park Professional Center**
**1700 West Walnut Avenue, Suite A**
**Visalia, CA 93277**

**Phone: 800-524-6390**
**Fax: 559-625-4990**

**Web Site: www.tksystems.org**

ISBN: 0-9701398-2-9

Printed in the United States of America

PROFIT FROM CHANGE

# Acknowledgments

*Profit from Change* could not have been completed without the help of family members, friends, and professional associates, all of whom helped to shape my work into a book I hope readers will find compelling and immediately useful.

Among those whose contributions I would specifically like to acknowledge are: BJ Anderson, who has been my discussion partner, daily editor, and all-around good friend; Laura Belgrave, for her creative input and final edit; Jim Pietras, for his graphic design work; the staff at Troy Korsgaden Insurance in Visalia, California – the "Ultimate High-Performance Team"; Sharon Jansma, my office director and "leader of the band"; Iva Korsgaden and Janette Somera at TKSystems, for all their hard work; my family – especially Michael and Emily, who unconditionally love their dad; and finally, all the agents, their staff, managers and company executives who have supported me in my effort to provide systems and information to the insurance industry.

Thank you, one and all. Your help and encouragement have meant more than you can know.

*Troy Korsgaden*

PROFIT FROM CHANGE

# Change Ripples through Our Industry

Over the last couple of years I've enjoyed the opportunity of meeting thousands of managers and agents, and I've had intense discussions with them about the continued viability of the agent-based distribution model. What is the value proposition of doing business with an insurance agent, and how many agents provide full value? Does the customer perceive any difference in value between insurance companies that work directly with customers and those that use agents? Ask insurance agents these questions and most get defensive. Ask company executives and, off the record, most express frustration in dealing with agents, specifically with the agent's inability to adapt to a changing environment. Talk about tension!

Of even greater significance, however, is a revolution going on at the customer level. With 24/7 access to the Internet, customers are more informed than ever in their dealings with insurance agents. More importantly, after being burned repeatedly by companies in all industries that over-promise but under-deliver, customers today are more wary—even cynical. Their skepticism has been fueled by the accounting scandals that engulfed some of the largest companies in America. You don't need a Quija Board to spell out the crisis of trust that surrounds not only those companies, but by now has leached into a lot of our biggest institutions. Fair or not, that's just the way it is.

Ironically, though, customers need more help today than ever before. Never mind great new technology and instant access to information. Today's reality is that people's lives are more stressful than ever, and as a result, time has surpassed money as their most precious commodity. It's a new dynamic altogether. But pair that dynamic with the prevailing atmosphere of distrust, and you quickly see how the combination has thrown existing customer relationships with any business into jeopardy.

Regrettably, our own industry isn't immune. In fact, our industry has been altogether too slow to respond to the changing perceptions of customers. It's even evident in the vocabulary we use. Think about the word "claim," for instance. We use it to describe an event that triggers the fulfillment of the promise we made to our customers when they established a contractual relationship with us. Add to that what we call the people we've assigned to help customers resolve their problems: claims adjusters. Talk about adversarial signals! We're off to a bad start even before we get out of the chute.

We can also see the industry's need for change in how agents evaluate their own success. Agents are ranked by PIF (policies-in-force) or total premium, not by customers. The life insurance commission structure frontloads commissions, encouraging agents to ignore their customers once the sale is made. Is it any wonder that the growth rate of insurance companies is consistently in the single digits? Imagine what would happen to our industry if a customer-focused company entered the marketplace.

As these changes in consumer perception ripple through our industry, we all seem to blame each other for their cumulative effect instead of working together to adapt to new challenges. This disconnect is why I decided to write this book. I believe that agents are uniquely positioned to capitalize on the changing nature of the customer because the customer is looking for a relationship with someone he or she can trust. In the new environment, the power of the individual relationship will separate the winners from the losers. Agents have a huge head start in this environment because they are local and trusted.

The agency-distribution system, with all its flaws, is not going away anytime soon, primarily because agents continue to deliver what insurance companies want and need—product sales. More importantly, agents are local, accessible, and can offer the human touch while giving customers what they want—peace of mind when it comes to asset protection and accumulation. Can agents do a better job of interacting with their customers? Yes, and I'll show you how.

Meanwhile, many companies are exploring direct-selling approaches to keep costs down and try new avenues of product distribution. Given their mandate to deliver the best possible bottom-line results to their shareholders, it's not hard to understand their strategy. And, in fact, the direct-selling approach, which typically relies on call centers, may result in the short term with new product sales. That's especially true if sales are based on the lowest prices. But have these companies really satisfied their goal of gaining *long-term* business? No.

I believe that after reading this book you will see why the agency-distribution system is here to stay and why the opportunity is better than it's ever been. However, we need to change the way we deal with our customers.

*Profit from Change* provides a road map for agents and companies to follow to adapt and profit from the transitions taking place around us. But before you can, you must believe in your own heart that you have to change. I spend the first part of this book explaining why. In Part Two I show you how to change to better serve your customers. Part Three I devote to successful systems you can use to retool your agency to become more customer-centric and therefore profitable. Part Four discusses the future opportunities you can embrace once you have retooled your agency.

I'm convinced there has never been a better time to be an agent or to own an insurance agency. Remember, people want to deal with people they know and trust. If we all take the next step and become more customer-focused in order to seal our relationships and cement that trust, I believe the agency-distribution model will maintain its superiority as the model to use in the insurance and financial services industries. Walk with me. I'll show you how.

— *Troy Korsgaden*

# Table of Contents

# Appendix One

## EXHIBIT A

## EXHIBIT B

## EXHIBIT C

# Appendix Two

## EXHIBIT A

# Appendix Three

## EXHIBIT A

## EXHIBIT B

Six Marketing Letters

## EXHIBIT C

## EXHIBIT D

## EXHIBIT E

PROFIT FROM CHANGE

# PART ONE

# THE INSURANCE INDUSTRY IN THE 21ST CENTURY

PROFIT FROM CHANGE

# THE GLASS IS FULL
## CHAPTER | ONE

It's an age-old question we all contemplate at one time or another: Is my glass half empty or half full? On any given day you can probably tick off a dozen problems with our industry and your own agency. We all can. If you choose to focus on that, your glass is half full.

On the same day, I'm sure you can also find as many or more reasons why there has never been a better time to be in this business. That's seeing the glass as not only half full, but overflowing.

Of course, if you look at a glass of water from far away, it's hard to tell if it's full or empty. In other words, many of us don't realize how good we've got it. At the end of the day, ours is a business based on trust, nothing more, nothing less, and that can't be measured by traditional Wall Street standards. That's why we continue to beat out the sophisticated Wall Street guys.

For over 30 years, the Wall Street big shots have tried an end-run around the agency-based distribution channel. First it was 1-800-CHEAP INSURANCE. Then it was the Internet. These direct writers scoffed at the agency-based distribution channel. They believed it was inefficient and too expensive. They assumed the only thing customers really wanted was the cheapest auto or homeowners insurance they could find. From their perspective, insurance has been nothing but a necessary evil and a commodity product. And sure, they did pick up some market share with their thinking, but it's no secret that they've hit a plateau with nothing near a dominant share of the industry.

So here we are, 30-plus years later, and agents are still king. Why? Because we're in a business based on TRUST! People will pay extra for knowing that you, the agent, will be there to take care of them when an accident or tragedy occurs. It's hard to get that feeling dialing an anonymous 1-800 number. Even though most of your customers deal with you over the phone and not face to face, they still know you're there. You're not in your office for 24 hours a day—they get that; they understand—but what matters to them is your accessibility. You're part of their local community. You have a name they know. Simply put, they can find you. It gives them peace of mind.

## THE HUMAN SPIRIT

*A good friend of mine who owns a successful insurance agency in Oklahoma tells agents "don't worry about computers or impersonal direct marketing." Why? Because, as he points out, there are two things a computer can't do: First, he says, "A computer has a hard time pivoting to another sale," and, second—most importantly—"A computer can't have the human spirit."*

Being local is definitely a competitive advantage. But it's not the only one. Take a look at what's going on around you. We live in an age of accelerating change, from technological advances to breakthroughs in medicine. They're all changes that have had a huge impact on our lives.

Today you can sit at home, pay your bills online, watch a first-run movie on your television with surround-sound, surf the web, communicate with your best friends—wherever they live—and you can do it all instantly. Technology is making it easier for us to cocoon.

Then there are advances in biotechnology, such as the discovery of new drugs that can prolong life. Did you know that if you live to age 65 you have a 50 percent chance of making it to your 90th birthday? Think about that. Not only are most of us are going to live longer, but it's entirely possible we'll be retired for as long as we worked!

It's an amazing environment, but ask people about their lives today and most say they don't have enough time to do everything they want to do. It's a Catch-22. Here we are, with more and better tools with which to control what we can do, but we have less time to do what we want to do. You probably feel the same way. That's why, when asked about your business and prospects for the future, it's natural to see the glass as half empty instead of overflowing.

But it bears repeating: There has never been a better time to be an insurance agent. As our world has grown more complex, as big corporate scandals have shaken our faith in Wall Street and the political system, our psyche has been forever changed. We've been burned, and clever ads don't con us any longer. That's true of your customers as well. They want what you want—something they can touch and feel. In the insurance and financial services industry, that's you, the local and trusted professional.

I'm not here to tell you that customers don't evaluate price, convenience, knowledge and superior service when they're evaluating insurance or financial products. They do. Of course they do. But in the end, the competitive advantage you have is the personal relationship you develop with your customers. In other words, as in the childhood game of tag, you are "it."

## The Need for Someone Like You

Remember, in the chaotic and time-deprived atmosphere we all live in, customers need personal advisors more than ever. They might get down-and-dirty price quotes from the Internet, but that's about where it stops. The Internet certainly can't help them evaluate value. No matter how sophisticated a web site, and no matter how many megabytes of memory a computer has, neither can explain the choices and impact of various types of coverage or financial products. That means the Internet can never be a trusted advisor. It's a problem for customers, because most don't know enough about the details of insurance, the law, or their potential liability to make intelligent buying decisions without the help of an informed professional—you.

## EVERY FILE IS A BEATING HEART

*I was visiting an agency in California a few years ago, and while waiting to meet with the agent I started talking to one of his customer service representatives. She was having a tough day dealing with some customers but she never became unglued. "How do you stay so positive?" I asked. She responded by pointing to the file cabinets that lined the wall. "Every file is a beating heart and everyone on the phone is trying to get through life. My job is to make our customers' lives easier."*

True, changes in the industry and new competition require us to formulate new strategies to compete effectively and win business. The power of the personal relationship is the key advantage we offer. Yet how are you leveraging this advantage? Do you know the names of each person you insure? Do you measure your agency's success by the number of policies-in-force, or by the number of customers with whom you have a personal relationship? Do you focus on selling just one or two lines of insurance instead of meeting all the needs of your customers? Sadly, many of the most successful agencies today resemble direct-writer shops with lots of staff handling the phones, high employee turnover, and have an impersonal feel. Although this approach may be an attractive short-term business model, it will ultimately fail. Why? Because there is no compelling value proposition anchoring the customer to the agency.

# Banish Old Ways of Thinking

Have you heard or made this comment recently: "Competition is coming out of the woodwork and it's killing me on price," or, "If things don't change soon the flood of policies leaving by the back door is going to put my agency under." Rumors of the demise of the agency-distribution system are greatly exaggerated and generally come from agents who are unwilling to adapt to a changing marketplace. Many of these same agents are frozen by fear; fear that they'll suffer the same fate as dinosaurs—extinction!

## OPPORTUNITIES ABOUND FOR ALL AGENTS

It was less than 20 years ago when all of the major insurance companies advised their independent distribution centers (agents) to transform from salespersons to business owners. Did every agent make the change? Some did, but many did not. Remember the days when there were clearly defined boundaries between insurance agencies, banks, and brokerage houses? They're gone! With the 1999 repeal of Glass-Steagall, Depression-Era national legislation that created those barriers, the lines of demarcation have blurred. Today, companies are focused on retention and organic growth, and many have formed strategic alliances. For the personal insurance professional this is nothing short of the next gold rush, not seen since the 1850s in California.

So why are the majority of insurance and financial services professionals waiting on the sidelines to strike the mother lode? Perhaps it's because the change isn't what they had planned. Great opportunities rarely meet you on the same path. Instead you must recognize the opportunity on a new course, in a new direction. You can do it, but you have to embrace change first. You have to become an evangelist of change. Look around your agency every day and find something you can change for better results. Write it down, then next to it write down the date that you'll initiate the change. When that day comes, just do it! And don't worry; I'll be giving you loads of strategies to help you get there.

In the process of writing this book I had the great fortune to talk to thousands of personal insurance agents and witness firsthand the transformation of agencies all across the country. Many agents have made a conscious choice to take an offensive stance rather than playing defense. These agents are redefining their roles as personal insurance and financial services professionals, and adapting to new market conditions. They're leveraging their greatest single asset—a personal relationship based on trust. That's what this book is all about, because those personal relationships are the landmarks on a road map to the future.

In the pages that follow I'll define the opportunity, show you how to exploit the obvious, and help you lay a foundation for the greatest business opportunity of your lifetime.

## Your Success Depends on You

If you're willing to give 100 percent to make your agency a success and if you follow the system that I detail in the following pages you will succeed. But first ask yourself some difficult questions. Am I ready? Am I enthusiastic about changing my agency? Am I ready to change my life and the way I view my business? Am I ready to put the fun back into what I do? Am I willing to get recharged and fully engaged in what I do for a living? If you answered a resounding "Yes!" then you're ready to join me for this incredible journey.

Congratulations! You've decided to become part of the future instead of the past, so let's get started. It's time to take a closer look at that glass of water!

# Chapter Highlights

— As a personal insurance agent you already have a competitive advantage over other distributors of insurance products—a personal relationship with your customers.

— Consumers need a personal advisor for their own protection. They won't get that from 1-800-CHEAP INSURANCE. They will get it from you.

— Change is inevitable, so banish your old ways of thinking and profit from it!

— Clearly defined boundaries between insurance, banking, and financial services are gone. Adapt to today's realities to guarantee yourself a seat at the distribution table.

PROFIT FROM CHANGE

# TAKE A NEW LOOK AT YOURSELF—AND YOUR CUSTOMERS

# CHAPTER TWO

Insurance agents can generally be divided into three groups. The first group is comprised of agents who are always on the lookout for new ways to run their businesses more efficiently and productively. They're the high achievers, willing to change the status quo to become even more successful. They're also the early adaptors, and you can count on them to seize the day when a new opportunity arises. When the prospect of selling banking services and investment products became a reality, for instance, the early adaptors were first in line to recognize the value in those possibilities—and to market financial services to customers.

The second group includes agents who are successful, but conservative about embracing change. I call this group "the thinkers." They typically "think it over" until the early adaptors prove that a new opportunity is worthwhile. Then—and only then—are they willing to make the necessary investment and capitalize on the opportunity.

The third group is made up of "the cautious" agents. They're the ones who tend to see the water glass as half empty. They're reluctant to adjust to market changes, and say things like, "We've always done it this way," or, "I don't want to take the risk." While they may not be totally satisfied with their lot in life or their level of success, they have no greater ambition than to conduct business as usual, even if they miss out on opportunities along the way.

Of these three categories, which group do you think will still be in business in five years? I firmly believe the answer is all of group one, most of group two, and a few of group three.

My primary reason for describing the three groups of agents is to highlight your need to believe you can alter the way you view your customers, how you think about your agency, and your overall attitude and enthusiasm for the insurance business. If you're willing to change, I make you this promise: You can take charge of your future. Experience has shown me that opportunities are gifts and that it's foolish to decline such treasures.

## Become an Evangelist of Change

Today's early adaptors are the insurance industry's evangelists of change. They charge down a new path, learning as they go. These courageous agents are reaping the rewards of serving more of their customers' needs while vastly improving their revenue stream. You, too, can become an evangelist of change, and there are lots of reasons for doing so: Your business will grow, your customers will be happier and more loyal, your income will be larger, and your agency will not only survive, but prosper.

The old way of doing things was to sell insurance products to as many people as possible. For multi-line agents this typically included auto insurance and homeowners insurance. Agents on the cutting edge would also sell life insurance or establish some commercial accounts.

The new way of thinking is to focus on the needs of your customers. What products do they want? What products do they need? It doesn't take a mental giant to figure out that you can sell more products to your existing customers when you know what they need. But you won't know what your customers want until you start talking with them. Find out what their needs are and learn to match a product that addresses those needs. The insurance business is no longer about selling policies. It's about what you can do for your customers. What a concept!

## STAY FOCUSED ON
## FILLING CUSTOMER NEEDS

*The owner of a small, fast-growing agency on the West Coast shares his thoughts: "I learned many valuable lessons in learning how to refocus my agency, using my time and energy to be customer-focused instead of product-focused. One of the most important things that's helping my agency grow is systematizing appointment scheduling. This gives me the opportunity to spend the majority of my time meeting with clients and getting to know their needs. I want to stay up to date with the needs of my customers and continually build the relationship. And my customers need the 'face' time to feel safe, secure, and sleep well at night."*

## Customers Don't Care about the Transaction

For years this industry has been focused on the "transaction." We sold an auto policy—a transaction. We sold a homeowners policy—another transaction. That might work for the agent, but does the customer really care about "the transaction?" Of course not. What John Q. Customer wants is excellent service, knowledge that the product he purchased "delivers," convenience, and someone he can trust to go to for answers. As an insurance professional your job is to protect your customers' assets now and in the future, and to help build them. If you can do this, you'll be successful. Delivering anything less is just baloney!

So much of what we do appears complicated and confusing to customers. Take auto insurance, for example. One of the reasons auto insurance has yet to take off on the Internet is that most consumers are confused by the specifics. First of all, they have to wade through perplexing terms such as "limits of liability," "deductibles," "limits," and "riders"— buzzwords that few consumers fully understand, and no wonder! It's our jargon, not theirs! Second, there's no one in cyberspace who can help them isolate what they really need. What they thought would be a convenience when they got online to ferret out some information turned into a fat waste of time. Unfortunately, the same thing sometimes happens in face-to-face encounters between agents and prospective customers. The good news is that it doesn't have to if you're dealing with your customers using a needs-based approach.

Let's take another look at explaining auto insurance, only this time using a needs-based method and ditching the jargon. Say you've got a customer who's just come to you for a low quote. That's hardly unusual. But is the lowest price really what your customer is looking for? Is it the only thing? No. What he wants is a product that lets him get in his car every day and not have to worry if he winds up in an accident. Your explanation might go something like this:

*"I can give you just a low-price quote, but it may leave you exposed if something happens. Instead, let me ask you several questions to identify the coverage that will enable you to get in your car every day and not have to guess whether you're really protected."*

It's a straightforward, easy-to-understand explanation, and it opens the door to some real dialogue. So if you think you have the upper hand by spewing forth gobbledygook insurance lingo, stop it! Start thinking about providing customers what they really want—one place to do business, someone easy to do business with, and peace of mind.

Break out of that limiting box labeled "insurance salesperson." See the larger opportunity and see the big picture—the true picture. That picture is of the household, and what products and services you can provide that best serve not only the needs of a particular customer, but the needs of the customer's entire household. It's such a vital component of profiting from change that the next chapter is focused on it.

## Customer-Focused Growth

Product-focused managers at the corporate home office like to talk about growing individual product lines. Their entire mission is to sell more and more of the products they manufacture each year. In fact, they're so focused on product sales that many have lost touch with the people they're selling to. Don't let that happen to you. A more successful approach is to identify the needs of your customers first, and concentrate on finding the products that fit those needs. The sales will follow.

## PUT THE CUSTOMER FIRST—NO MATTER WHO THE CUSTOMER IS

*After 22 years of owning and operating an insurance and financial services agency, I can honestly say, "I have seen it all." Accounts come in all shapes and sizes. However, the philosophy in my agency is that every person deserves the same level of attention and service. Everybody's money is green. And no matter what the dollar amount, that transfer of funds buys them the type of service they desire and have every right to expect. We don't service policies, we don't service premium; we just service people. We get paid for the value we bring at the end of the day. Put another way, instead of worrying about the specific transaction, we focus on the sum total of our service.*

I guarantee that as you adopt a customer-focused approach you will revitalize your business. It's no longer dialing for dollars or even X-dating. In fact—and don't panic—I believe that as you adopt a customer-focused approach, the number of customers you serve could actually shrink. But that's not bad news, because the number of products per customer will increase significantly.

Look, why did you decide to become an insurance agent? Did someone promise you that if you worked hard for five years, you would be able to coast for the rest of your career on renewal commissions? Did you fall into the insurance business because you weren't doing anything else at the time or were frustrated with what you were doing? Did you want to be your own boss and make a lot of money? Did you always want to be an agent?

Whatever your reasons, what I've found is that too many agents are frustrated, bored, and uninspired with running their agencies. Some flatly dislike what they do. They don't feel like they're adding value or making a difference. If you're one of those agents, don't despair, because if you can adapt to the changes that have impacted our industry—and you can—you can win big. And guess what? You'll find that your job has morphed into something you enjoy. In fact, when you make your daily goal one of helping your customers, you'll find that your job is downright invigorating.

## The Big Changes

So what's been going on? As I described in Chapter One, technology, access to information, and constraints on time have changed the typical consumer. Consumers know more, they expect more, and they're less forgiving. You're no longer the only game in town and you can no longer sell on price because the direct writers will beat your rates. So how do you compete? You have to provide value so your customer can justify paying more.

Take a look at retail clothing for an example of the success of customer-focused growth. Nordstrom department store has had phenomenal success by delivering high-quality service. Sales associates are trained to put the needs of the customer first, ahead of making a sale. Are their prices higher? Yes, but thousands of people enjoy shopping there.

## HOW I CAME TO BUY A PINK SHIRT

*I was at a shopping mall recently and found a silk tie I especially liked at Macy's. It was a busy shopping day and the line to the cashier was long, so I headed down to Nordstrom to check out the tie selection there. Sure enough, Nordstrom had the same tie, but it was more expensive. A sales associate immediately approached me and commented how great the tie looked with my jacket and mentioned that the store had just received a new shipment of dress shirts that would make a perfect ensemble. So I not only bought the more expensive tie, but a new pink shirt as well. What a pleasant buying experience! Sure, I paid more, but the personal service and convenience of the transaction made it worthwhile. I will pay more for quality and excellent service every time.*

I guarantee that as you adopt a customer-focused approach you'll feel revitalized. Why? Because your business will be based on filling customer needs. It's a subtle but powerful change in how you think about what you do every day.

# Chapter Highlights

— There are three categories of agents: the early adaptors, the thinkers, and the super cautious. Which are you?

— Become an "evangelist of change." The early adaptors are winning big because they discovered a new way of thinking. It's about what you can do for your clients.

— Ditch the insurance jargon, and use a needs-based approach in helping your customers truly understand what they need to be protected.

— Customer-focused growth is a strategy to sell more products to existing customers, thereby filling more of their needs.

# LEVERAGE THE
OPPORTUNITIES
YOU SEE

CHAPTER | THREE

You already know you need to embrace change and start seeing your customers differently, beginning with a needs-based approach. But maybe at this point you're saying to yourself, "All right, fine. A needs-based approach sounds feasible, and it certainly serves my customers. I even buy into the idea that I'll find the process energizing. But, well . . . how exactly does my agency actually profit from all that?"

**Answer:** You learn to leverage the opportunities that you already have by taking a holistic view. It's a mind set, really. Each customer lives in a household. That household could be made up of just one person, two people, or an entire family. The people in the household could be related or not. Society has changed. Households are now diverse. It really doesn't matter. What's important is how much information you have about the household and its inhabitants. Let's look at both typical and atypical households. You'll quickly see where those opportunities lay.

## HOUSEHOLD #1

The Johnson household is traditional, consisting of a married couple with two children. They live in a house and have a mortgage. Both spouses work outside the home, so each adult has an auto. The children are 12-year-old Melissa and 16-year-old Scott. You know the Johnsons like to water ski and own a ski boat.

Using just this basic information, you can begin to determine the Johnson family's insurance needs. They need homeowners insurance, they need an auto policy on two cars, they need a policy on their boat, they need life insurance on both adults, and they may need an umbrella policy. They also need a college savings plan for both children, and they need to save for retirement. Scott will be driving soon, which means they'll need additional coverage for that as well.

This is where the change in how you think about your customers comes into play. You have to look at what the customer needs for his household instead of looking at just the existing policies. It's a total reversal in how you regard your customer. Looking at the Johnson household in its entirety, what is the potential for insurance and financial services products? Count them up:

- 1 homeowners policy
- 2 auto policies
- 1 umbrella policy
- 1 boat policy
- 2 life insurance policies
- 2 college savings plans
- 2 IRAs

Minimal potential: 11 products

Other possibilities include life insurance for the children, disability insurance for the parents, health insurance for the family, and, as you learn more about the Johnsons, you may discover additional needs such as insurance on jewelry, furs, and so on.

## HOUSEHOLD #2

The Smith household is upper-middle class. Mr. Smith owns an electrical contracting business with 10 employees. Mrs. Smith is a homemaker busy with three active children: Justin, age 10, Jennifer, age 4, and Jeremy, age 2. The family owns a vacation cabin in the mountains, two cars, and a boat.

Even though you don't have much information on this household, it's easy to determine the family's basic needs:

- 2 homeowners policies
- 1 umbrella policy
- 2 auto policies
- 1 boat policy
- 2 life insurance policies on the two adults
- 3 life insurance policies for the children
- 3 college savings plans
- 1 retirement savings plan

— 1 commercial policy for the business

— Insurance to cover the business's trucks

— Workers' comp for the employees

— Disability insurance on Mr. Smith as the sole breadwinner

Minimal potential: 19 products

Does Mr. Smith's business have a 401(k) plan for its employees? There may be potential to write insurance on each of the employees and their households. The possibilities just keep multiplying and multiplying. You're starting to get the picture.

## HOUSEHOLD #3

This household consists of two working professionals in their early thirties: John Jackson, a physician, and his live-in partner Mary Bennett, a computer systems consultant. They own a home together and each has a luxury automobile.

Their household needs:

— 2 auto insurance policies

— 1 homeowners policy

— 2 life insurance policies

— An investment plan for retirement

— An umbrella policy

Minimal Potential: 7 products

If you think beyond the basics, you'll also see that Mary needs additional coverage on the computer equipment in her home office, and Dr. Jackson needs insurance for his medical practice and workers' comp for his employees.

That's just the beginning. This couple could be an excellent referral source to your agency from their peer group, so the potential for add-on business is excellent.

## HOUSEHOLD #4

Take a look at the household of Penelope White and her two children, Michele, age 5, and Jonathan, age 7. Also sharing the household is Jim Carrington and his 10-year-old son Peter. Both adults work outside the home, they rent a house, and each adult has an auto to commute to work. What is the potential in serving the needs of this household?

— 1 renters insurance policy

— 2 auto policies

— 3 investment plans for college savings for three children

— 2 investment plans for retirement

— 2 life insurance policies

— 2 disability policies

Minimal potential: 12 products

These example households are presented to spark your thinking about the potential in your own database of customer information—and how to better analyze that information. I'll help you do that in the following chapters, but even now, start thinking about how well you really know your customers. Do you know how they spend their leisure time? Do you know the names and ages of their children? Life changes, people change, they get married, they get divorced, they have children, they start businesses, they start a new career, the children grow up. All of these events trigger a change in the needs of that household. If you're current with your customers you can capitalize on the possibilities and truly serve their needs.

## The Deeper Penetration Approach

Now that you've seen how sales opportunities can multiply when you peer into each household with an all-encompassing view, take a look at what happens when you run some simple numbers based on patterns in our industry. For instance, it used to be that every household had the potential for seven sales. But as demonstrated in the previous examples, today's households are much more diverse than in the past. That's good news for us, because with all that diversity, the potential for sales has expanded to 10— at least. For an agency with 1,000 households, that means it has the potential for 10,000 new sales in its existing book of business.

Now take into account that our industry's "hit ratio"—the average number of people you can sell to if you see them under the right conditions—is 20 percent. Do the math and you'll see that the hit ratio factored with the potential means our 1,000-household agency can score an additional 2,000 policies in its book of business. The agency doesn't have to drum up new customers to gain those sales. It only has to seize the opportunities that are already there. That agency? It could be yours.

## What About Single-Policy Households?

Savvy agents are putting their energy into areas where the greatest return exists, and that's clearly in the multi-policy household. They've learned that single-policy households simply aren't cost efficient. That's not to say that agents are abandoning mono-line customers without an opportunity to turn them into something more, but they've elected not to spin their wheels endlessly. Eavesdrop on a savvy agent about single-policy households and you'll likely hear something like this: "We're going to give this single-policy household a year and a half, three opportunities, one every six months, to make an additional purchase. If they're not willing to meet with us, if they're not willing to discuss these other opportunities, then they're not sold on our agency. Therefore, we can't afford to market them the same way we do somebody who has several different products with us."

Here's an illustration of why it's more efficient to have 1,000 households with four policies each than 4,000 customers with one policy each. In either case it equals 4,000 PIF. With 4,000 customers your phone rings all day long. It costs you a lot to service their business. On the other hand, the higher product-density agency operates more efficiently and profitably because one phone call services all four policies.

Your enduring challenge, of course, is to deepen the relationship with each of your customers, and clearly that includes your mono-line customers. But as you increasingly address the challenge, it's possible that one day you may come to the point where you decide that having a single-policy household no longer fits your business model at all. First you have to identify which customers don't want to grow with you, and in Chapter Nine I outline the process to make that assessment quickly and efficiently. What you'll probably discover is that a small percentage of your customers are content to have just one product with you, probably because you offered the lowest price at the time of purchase. Those are price-driven customers, which means they'll leave your agency at the drop of a lower price. Obviously you'll want to try and persuade them to expand their relationship with you, and you'll want to continue serving their accounts with the professionalism all of your customers deserve. In the end, though, price-driven customers are poor investments and if they signal their intent to disengage from your agency, let them. The days of clinging to customers who care only about price are over.

Now that you're beginning to look at your customers differently, in the next chapter I'll take you through the steps necessary to look at your agency differently. Is it geared up and staffed up to capitalize on today's opportunities? It's not that difficult to make it so, and I'll show you how.

# Chapter Highlights

— Today's business environment requires a holistic view: that we see the potential each household offers.

— Life is always changing. To maximize the potential in every household, stay on top of the major transitions in your customers' lives. What they need today could expand tomorrow.

— Gone are the days when households offered the potential for only seven sales. Today, the industry average is 10. Take advantage of it.

— Don't spend a disproportionate amount of time with single-policy customers who refuse to grow with you. You want customers who are driven by more than price and will respect the needs-based approach you bring to them.

PROFIT FROM CHANGE

# PART TWO

# REPOSITIONING YOUR AGENCY

PROFIT FROM CHANGE

# TAKING THE
# FIRST STEPS

CHAPTER | FOUR

Most of us were recruited into the insurance industry with the same line: "Work really hard for five years and you can live off your renewals and referrals for the rest of your career." That's how it worked in the early days, but it no longer does because the current marketplace demands that you operate your agency like a business. And if your business isn't growing, it's dying. In this chapter I'll take you through the steps and strategies to position your agency for consistent growth.

First, answer the following questions honestly (just between you and you):

— Am I an order taker or a business owner? Many agents fail to recognize that they operate a business.

— Am I proactive or reactive? Many agents sit and wait for business. They don't aggressively pursue new opportunities or avenues of growth.

— Do I worry about whether my accounts are growing? Am I keeping my customers?

If deep down inside you know that your agency is not growing, then it's time to take your first step: Commit to do something every day to increase sales in your agency.

# Breaking through to the Mother Lode

After years of studying agencies from one end of the United States to the other, I have two observations. The first: Agents hit bedrock somewhere between 1,800 and 2,200 policies. It's at this point that agency owners stop or drastically reduce their investment in business growth. They fall into the trap of becoming servicing clerks for the company or companies they represent.

I certainly understand that they've been working their tails off to get to this level and may take a break to enjoy the fruits of their labor. But for the long haul, stopping isn't a rational business decision, and I have two reasons for saying that. First, my research indicates that newer agencies with less than 1,000 policies-in-force spend an average of 8 to 10 percent of annual revenues on marketing. Yet as the agency grows they keep spending the same dollar amount on marketing, instead of using a percentage of annual revenue as a barometer for budgeting. Consequently, dollars spent on marketing declines. So what typically happens? The rate of new business commission and annual growth slows or stops.

My second observation? Agents hit bedrock on staffing as well. Most say the reason is, "There just isn't enough revenue to support adding staff." They won't make the investment without knowing for certain that the investment will pay off. How do they evaluate making the investment? Their typical answer is a vague: "There isn't the same new business potential that there was when I got into the business." However, the important question these agents should ask is: "How much potential for add-on business is there in the households we already serve?" The risk isn't in adding another staff member—that would be a confident move—but in ignoring potential business that you already have. There will always be enough new business in the households you serve. In fact, your customer database is pure gold. The real secret is knowing how to extract the gold from it.

# The Agency Evaluation Worksheet

If you really want to mine through the bedrock to get to the mother lode you need to establish an exact point of entry, which means you have to survey the landscape. That requires you to take a holistic view of your agency, examining two things: where you spend your money, and which products generate income for your agency.

I've included the "Agency Evaluation Worksheet" in **Appendix One** to help you through this important step. It contains forms called "Annual Revenue by Product Line" and "Annual Agency Expenses." Fill everything out completely and be as precise as possible. When you're done with the worksheets, take time to answer the questions in "Learning from this Exercise" at the end. The questions will help you determine the health of your agency, and if you're like most agents you'll uncover some surprises. That's okay. There are no right or wrong answers. What you're doing is getting a snapshot of your agency as it exists today, the honest evaluation you need before you can take a leap to the next level.

You'll be amazed at how quickly you spot areas that need to change or can be tweaked for better results. To give you just one idea of the kinds of things you might realize when you finish your own evaluation, check out the sample agency I've presented at the end of "Learning from This Exercise." I've contrasted the bottom line of this sample agency with the bottom line it could be enjoying if it made just a few alterations. Start visualizing ways you could do the same.

## I SHOULD HAVE EVALUATED MY AGENCY YEARS AGO

*Even owners of large, successful agencies who go through the agency evaluation process discover better ways of running their businesses and find there is always room for improvement. One such example comes from the owner of a large agency in a metro area who told me, "This was a real eye-opener! Going through the agency evaluation process helped me look at my agency differently. I should have done this years ago. It's easy to fall into the trap of just doing business as usual. Now it's obvious to me that some changes need to be made, especially in marketing focus. Deeper penetration per household will balance out my book of business."*

In the next chapter I'll guide you through the essential next steps you need to take in order to realize your vision. Meanwhile, let's explore some truths about managing a successful business in today's marketplace.

# Profit Centers

Your insurance agency is a sales and marketing business and you must begin to look at it that way. By doing so, you cut through all the noise and get right to the bottom line of your agency.

How do you alter your approach? First, you must identify your profit centers. Basically, there are two types: profit centers generated from products, and profit centers generated from employees. Each product must be a profit center—period. Products that cost you more to market than you generate in revenues are not profitable. Every employee must be a profit center—period. Each employee must generate revenue for your agency greater than his or her compensation. Employees who don't are cost centers. You need to examine your cost centers and take action to convert them into profit centers. Let's look at this concept in more detail.

## PRODUCTS

If your agency is like the typical multi-line agency, a high per-centage of your revenue comes from the auto line of business. Indeed, a typical agency generates 50 percent of its revenue from auto. The impact can be significant. If an agent has a retention rate of 85 percent, that agent needs to replace 15 percent of his or her auto book of business every year just to stay even. How much staff time do you devote to auto service? Assign an annual dollar figure to that service. Does having 50 percent of your eggs in the auto basket still make sense? For the majority of agencies, a more balanced book of business is more profitable.

## EMPLOYEES

In most agencies the largest single expenditure is payroll. Most agents hire staff when the workload is more than they can handle, an approach I call "defensive hiring." Although there may be some small, incremental profits from defensive hiring, there aren't any quantum leaps in revenue because everyone is just doing a little bit more of the same.

On the other hand, by stepping back and viewing your agency as a business, you can define a course of action that leverages all of your assets, including your employees. Start by asking yourself whether each of them contributes to the agency's bottom line. Take a critical look. Do you have employees who do nothing but administrative or service work? If you do, they're not adding to your bottom line, plain and simple. Does that mean they aren't valuable? Of course not. Excellent service is obviously a foundation for your success. But unless you're content to march in place forever, your employees need to do more than answer phones and move paper, no matter how good they are at it. Today's rapid-fire business environment demands it, and if you want to grow your agency then you've got to take your employees to the next level. You need to get them to generate new revenue as well.

Remember, your business is no longer based on how many policies you can sell. Instead, it's based on providing your customers with peace of mind. The only way you're going to be able to identify what they ultimately need is for everyone in your office to come together to find out. The "back room" service that the customer may never see has to be seamless—from each customer service representative (CSR) in your office to underwriting and claims employees. You need to focus on every household in your agency. The customer needs to see your operation as one team, not disparate pieces of a complicated puzzle. That comes from a change in thinking. And when you do provide the safety, security, and peace of mind that your customers want, then the sales, the policies, and the assets under management will follow just as surely as day follows night.

Here's where a change in thinking can be profitable, beginning with the way you approach adding staff. For instance, when you hire people, make sure you're not adding them to your payroll strictly to do administrative work. Make certain they understand that driving revenue is the key to success, and that indeed, generating sales isn't an option, but an expectation. To avoid misunderstandings later, build it into your written job descriptions.

It bears repeating: Any employee who isn't a profit center is a cost center. But if you hire and train your employees to mine for opportunities, you'll soon see that the profits they generate are greater than the costs of keeping them on the payroll. In fact, as long as you structure your hiring process to ensure that each employee drives revenue, there really is no reason not to add staff now and in the future. Being proactive with your staff is part of a building-block system for constructing an agency with departments, each one a profit center.

## THE AGENCY OF THE FUTURE

*My view of how the agency of the future should be structured is based on my experience in working with thousands of agencies. Here is what I suggest: Hire employees for a specific product line, or as I call them, departments. The ultimate goal is to have an auto department, a fire department, a life department, a financial services department, a health department, etc. Of course, I recognize that the typical agent can't start out this way. It's a building process. You may want to start by building your auto department, staffed by an auto specialist (agency producer) and a CSR. Then hire a CSR who specializes in fire, and so on as you build. You'll learn more about the process for this in Chapter Seven.*

I'm not advocating that each of your employees needs to be a sales person in the conventional sense. What I am advocating is that you get each staff member to become an information gatherer and information giver, forever on a quest to learn as much as possible about your customers and their households. That's how they become profit centers, and the process is actually astonishingly simple. Let's look at an example. Say you've got a customer named Mr. Smith. He calls in to make a car change on his current policy. Mr. Smith mentions that he and his wife have traded in their four-year-old convertible for a new Chevy Suburban. Your CSR obtains the new car information as well as the lender's name and address for a binder. The service is both prompt and professional, and the customer is pleased. You're pleased with the CSR's performance as well.

But now let me show you the missed opportunity. Assume the same facts, except this time your CSR asks Mr. Smith why he bought a new car. He responds that with a toddler and a new child on the way, he and his wife needed to upgrade to a more family-oriented vehicle. Through a series of additional questions, the CSR is now able to suggest several products that can help the Smiths better manage their affairs. It all started with one friendly question. The CSR didn't bully her way to a sale. All she did was take a routine call one step further. That's an employee who's learned how to leverage a customer interaction instead of just focusing on processing paperwork. Imagine if all your employees did the same. They can, and I'll show you how in Chapter Ten.

First, though, if you're ready to develop an overall plan that'll put your agency in the driver's seat—and keep it there—cruise on into the next chapter. I've got a road map that'll point you to the express lanes and get you to your destination ahead of the competition.

# Chapter Highlights

— Many agents hit bedrock at 1,800-2,200 policies-in-force.
Overcome that obstacle by committing to change.

— Evaluate your agency as it exists today. Learn where you
spend your money, and which products generate income.

— Your products are profit centers. Through the agency
evaluation process pinpoint which of them contribute most
to your bottom line. Capitalize on the winners.

— Turn every employee into a profit center and watch your
revenue soar.

PROFIT FROM CHANGE

# CREATING A ROAD MAP FOR SUCCESS

# CHAPTER FIVE

At this point in your reading, you're already on your way to rethinking a lot of things. You're looking at your customers as more than one-shot prospects. You're viewing your agency as more than a one-stop shop. And you're beginning to see the potential in your employees as more than just a payroll expense each month. Good. Your glass is well past the half-mark point. Grab a pitcher; you're ready to fill that glass to the top.

## Ouch! The Business Plan

Maybe you cringe when you hear the words "business plan." I don't blame you. Those two little words always sound so daunting. In fact, I prefer to use the term "road map," because that's really what a business plan is. Business plans are maps designed to move your agency forward based on written goals that take advantage of what you've learned. Your road map doesn't have to be complicated. It doesn't have to be inflexible, and indeed, you should aim for something versatile enough to accommodate unexpected changes. But your road map does have to reflect concrete goals, and it does have to be written down. That's the first step. The second step is to develop an action plan, or what I call a "playbook," to get you from where you are to where you want to be. Reviewing your road map and playbook daily will not only drive you from Point A to Point B, but will help you sustain growth, even with the many changes that are sure to come in the insurance industry.

## ENERGIZED FOR LIFT-OFF GROWTH

*A good road map not only boosts revenue, but goes a long way toward energizing people. Here's what one agent told me: "This was the fun part—putting our road map into action. We repositioned our agency for more profitability and totally changed our marketing thrust. But first I shared the road map and my goals with our staff and got them all fired up, too. It's amazing how enthusiasm and teamwork have propelled our agency into rocket-like 'lift-off growth!' "*

Over the years I've worked with thousands of agents to create personal and business road maps for success, road maps that have been a major factor in their success. A well thought-out plan will keep you focused and assist you in creating profit centers in both your product offerings and your staff positions. You should include an operational plan with projected revenue and expenses that are associated with running the business.

My own experience has shown me that your road map should be simple to create and use, and that it should cover no more than three years. The business world moves too quickly to forecast beyond such a time frame.

However, don't be fooled by thinking that a three-year road map doesn't call for vigilance. I've learned that you should look at your road map at least once a day, and you need to be flexible enough so that you can make changes every 90 days. It's at that point you'll want to pause and redefine your strategy for running your business based on what you learned during the last 90 days.

Of course, if you're like most of us, one of the most intimidating components you're likely to face in creating a road map is defining a mission statement. To do that you have to ask yourself, "What exactly is my business philosophy?" But relax. You don't have to be Aristotle in order to express yourself adequately. In truth, your stated philosophy can be as simple as:

*"The [agency name] endeavors to serve the insurance and financial needs of our customers by adhering to high ethical standards and providing excellent service."*

If that strikes you as too minimal for a mission statement, feel free to expand on it. Perhaps you'd like to articulate the unique values you bring to running your business. The point is that all you really need to craft is a straightforward declaration of what your agency does, and what it stands for.

# Designing Your Road Map

To make your life easier, I've included a worksheet called "Sample Road Map to Growing Your Agency" in **Appendix One**. The worksheet establishes the format for a road map. To personalize it, all you have to do is figure out how big you want your business to be. It's as simple as that. Start with the tools I've provided, namely the Agency Evaluation Worksheet and the questions that follow. What needs to change? Which product lines would contribute to a stronger agency bottom line? Factor in these answers when developing your road map. All agencies are different. Agency owners have different interests and skills. Integrate those components into your agency plan as well. It's your agency. Make sure your road map reflects your values, your goals, and your vision for the future. The quick discussion points below can help you develop all of them.

## PRODUCT LINES

Focus on how quickly you want to grow and what product lines you will offer. There is no "one size fits all" strategy, so make sure your road map includes where you are now, what your immediate goals are, and your long-term growth projections. Be detailed. This is where you're setting your basic financial goals. Your efforts at this stage will ensure your ability to maintain profit centers within your agency.

## STAFFING GOALS

The most effective road maps include specific, targeted, and measurable goals for staffing. Pay special attention to the percentage of gross annual revenue spent on payroll. According to my research, the number should be around 30 percent. Typically, payroll is the largest expense in an insurance agency. Because of that, you should determine not only the appropriate number of employees for your agency, but also evaluate their productivity and how they contribute to your bottom line.

## BUY OR RENT?

I urge you to include in your road map a "buy versus rent" analysis. If your office is in an area where real estate prices are very high, buying a building might not seem possible. On the other hand, the cost of rent over a long period of time can be staggering and unpredictable. Whether you're in a metropolitan city or a rural area, give some consideration to this issue.

## TECHNOLOGY

Technology will continue to play a big role in your business, chiefly because it'll help you maximize the mining of information from your customer database. So embrace it. Learn how it can help you better manage your business, and spell out how you'll use it in your agency plan. Be flexible enough to include new innovations as they become available, but stop short of automatically grabbing the fanciest equipment on the market or the most recent software release. After all, most of us don't need Excel on steroids. The key is figuring out an appropriate system for your agency, which I discuss in greater detail in Chapter Six.

## FINE-TUNING EFFICIENCIES

Your road map should include a plan to fine-tune existing interoffice systems, or what I refer to as "efficiencies within your operation." Most successful businesses have viable systems to speed workflow. These systems include database management, data entry, customer relationship management, procedures for handling daily transactions, protocol for answering the telephones, and so on. Our industry has similar service needs and therefore agents should likewise continually look for ways to maintain and improve their own systems to enhance their businesses. You don't have to go it alone. The best agents learn from their peers and adopt systems that work well in other agencies.

## GRAPPLING WITH PROFIT PER PRODUCT

A key component of your road map is understanding the profit per type of product you sell. Through my own research, I've found easy ways to calculate the profit per product, which includes acquisition, cost of service per policy, and the like. You can make calculations for future growth when considering retention of existing policies, and additional policies that are added to a household. So where do you begin? Start with your most profitable "product." To do this you need to know the profit per policy of each of the product lines you sell. In my office, the staff uses a calculator to measure this important information.

## Following Your Road Map

Don't be fooled. Creating a road map will not automatically lead you to success. It's a starting point—and an essential one—but the ticket to getting you to where you want to go comes from the action steps in your playbook. They move you beyond generalities into the particulars. Thus, after your road map is completed, you need to create what I call the "agency playbook." In it you'll include action steps to use day by day to implement your road map. Don't be surprised at how exhilarating you'll find this part of the process. After all, you're putting your goals in motion! What you want is no mere pipe dream now. It's reality. (See **Appendix One, Exhibit C** for a detailed approach to putting your goals into action.)

### TAKING ACTION

*An agency owner in the South, who is also a huge football fan, shares his experience: "Based on your advice I added a section to our business plan that includes a day-to-day, month-to-month tactical plan of action. As you suggested, this has become our agency playbook, which keeps me and my staff focused on accomplishing what's important now. This alone has made all the difference in my agency's performance. I like the consistent growth. The momentum just keeps building and building!"*

Excited? You should be. Nervous? Don't be. Getting to the next level isn't something you're expected to do on your own. In fact, don't even try. To increase profits and achieve the goals in your road map, you must begin to delegate to staff members many of the responsibilities of operating your agency. You're the chief executive officer of your business now, responsible for the overall direction and flow of your company—not for the day-to-day and moment-to-moment activities. An effective CEO hires people to carry out the business goals that he or she sets. One of the biggest pitfalls is for an agent to build the agency around himself/herself as the prime revenue generator. If you're to add significant revenue to your business you have to understand that you can't be the largest sales producer in your agency. Does that mean I advocate that you stop selling and only manage? No, of course not. Selling and marketing are very important to the lifeblood of your business. Just remember to make sure that everyone on your payroll understands that part of the job is to bring income into your business. In this way you can truly leverage every employee and increase agency income potential.

# WHAT IF I DON'T
# ALREADY HAVE A STAFF?

Even in today's competitive market, we are blessed. You don't need a lot of up-front capital to launch an insurance agency business. You don't have to hire a big staff immediately, as you would if you purchased a franchise or another more capital-intensive business. So yes, it's easy to get started in this business, but that doesn't mean you should take the ride alone. In fact, one of the questions I get asked all the time is: "When do I hire my first employee?" The answer is NOW, immediately!

## "I WAS FLYING BY THE SEAT OF MY PANTS"

*An agency owner in a Midwestern community told me, "I had never written a business plan for my agency. Now I see that I was just flying by the seat of my pants and had no control over my own business. I had never considered adding staff until we were all totally stressed out from overwork. Now I understand that in order to grow, I need to plan ahead. My plan includes benchmarks that take the guesswork out of 'when to hire.' For the first time in years, I feel like I'm in control, and the business is running much smoother and growing by leaps and bounds. I'm actually having fun again."*

Put another way: If you're spending any time at all providing service to customers instead of selling, it's time to hire an employee. If you're on the phone setting your own appointments, it's time to hire an Agency Contact Representative (ACR). You can be sure Bill Gates didn't get to be one of the richest men in the world by being too timid to add staff. Don't you be timid, either. Your valuable time needs to be spent in face-to-face sales meetings with prospects and clients. When you're designing your road map, consider the staff positions you'll need to free you from the drudgery work, and then build action steps into your playbook so you won't get sidetracked from following through.

## How Many Employees?

It used to be generally accepted that you needed to hire a staff person at X-number of policies. My own research shows that a staff person is typically hired for every 800 to 1,000 policies. But don't let PIF influence your decisions. That was yesterday's thinking. Today's thinking has to be driven by putting the customer first. Change your agency to reflect a focus on building high-density households. Determine when to hire a new employee based on the number of households you aspire to serve, not the number of policies you have in force. Remember, you service people, not PIF. Rather than worry about when to hire, use the facts, demographics, and past experience reflected in your Agency Evaluation Worksheet to determine the number of employees for your agency.

# Nothing Is Cast in Stone

Your agency runs the risk of stagnating if you don't have a viable internal system in place to take the guesswork out of day-to-day operations. You want a system so strong that using it almost becomes second nature for you and your staff, thereby speeding your agency's workflow and efficiency. If you're approaching the creation of your road map properly, you're designing that viable system to begin with, and you're building a playbook to make it work. Remember, though, that nothing is cast in stone, and you shouldn't be surprised or dismayed if you need to tweak your system from time to time. Modifications are fine. In fact, you'll recall that your road map calls for you to evaluate your strategy every 90 days. Maybe you'll find nothing to change. Maybe you'll find one or two areas you'll want to alter. That's the beauty of your road map. It's engineered for flexibility.

## EVEN A SINGLE CHANGE CAN BE HUGE

*The owner of a mid-sized agency told me, "We needed to upgrade our technology for smoother workflow. Wow! That one thing has made a huge difference! I hired a computer specialist to ensure that staff training went smoothly, too. My road map plan is working great!"*

You've made lots of progress if you have taken the steps I suggested in this chapter. You've put together a road map for success and an agency playbook that will help turn your vision into a reality. Good job! Stay with it!

However, this is only the beginning. In the next chapter I talk in detail about making the best use of technology. It doesn't have to cost you an arm and a leg. What it will do is help you mine your customer database to catapult you to the next level of success.

# Chapter Highlights

— Running a business is like taking a trip. It can be a pleasant, enjoyable experience or it can be fraught with danger if you're driving blind. Create a road map that will keep you focused on getting from point A to point B. Neglect this step at your peril.

— Put your road map into action with an agency playbook. Doing so will help keep you focused.

— Don't be afraid to hire! It's the only way to generate additional income and to profit from change.

— Use your road map to set up internal systems that quicken workflow and help your employees be more productive. Evaluate those systems regularly—and stay flexible!

PROFIT FROM CHANGE

# USE TECHNOLOGY FOR A LIGHTNING-SPEED OPERATION

# CHAPTER SIX

In the preceding chapters I've described the mindset and systems you need to profit from the changes going on in our industry and in society as a whole. But if you want to improve your results then you need a solid understanding of how best to use the technology available to you today. Trying to move your agency forward without it would be like using your thumb to hammer a nail to the wall.

One caveat before I begin: On its own, technology—and by that I mean the hardware, software, and peripherals you use to run your business—does nothing. Go to your computer, turn it on, and ask it to cross-sell your mono-line auto customers. Nothing will happen. Technology is merely a means to an end, a tool to assist you and your staff in driving more sales.

## Where to Start

Before you can evaluate whether you're making the best use of your technology, you have to know exactly what it is you want it to help you accomplish in your agency. In my view, it's all about enabling you to know as much as you can about your customers so you can provide them with better service and position yourself to identify cross-sell opportunities.

There are two ways you interact with your customers: (1) when they call your agency; (2) when you call them. Technology can tell you or your CSR all about the customer when he or she calls. It can also tell you when you should call your customer. Finally, it can provide information that allows your staff to access personal information about your customers, such as birthdays or anniversaries. Those might seem like trivial details, but bear in mind that acknowledging niceties highlights the personal nature of your customers' relationships with your agency and opens the door to more profitable dialogue.

Keeping in mind the goals for successful customer interactions and cross-selling opportunities, here are some of the specifics your technology should allow you to do:

— Swiftly access customer account information in order to accurately answer questions;

— Add or change customer information in real time;

— Process and record a transaction quickly and without errors;

— Focus on the customer, whether for sales or service, instead of administrative tasks;

— Create a database of customer information that you can leverage for future growth;

— Add and view customers notes;

— Send e-mail to customers, whether to just one or to a
segmented group;

— View forecasted sales, closed sales, and compare sales;

— Have instant access to team sales performance.

Your own needs or interests may be greater, but if your technology
lets you accomplish the basics outlined above, then you're in a
position to make it mine the gold in your database.

# What You Need

Do you have a computer in your office? Do your CSRs have
computers on their desks? Do they have printers close to their
desks so they don't waste time getting up and walking across the
office? Are your computers networked? Do you have a web site?
Do you communicate with your customers via e-mail? Do you
interact with your company electronically? These are some of
the questions you need to ask as you evaluate your agency's
technology position.

If you don't have a computer in your office, get one. If your computer isn't capable of running the latest version of your customer
relationship management software, it's time to upgrade to a faster

model. If you don't have a computer with Internet access, get it! And if you don't have a computer with high-speed cable or DSL access, upgrade and get that, too.

Don't overlook taking full advantage of the Internet. If you don't have a web site for your customers to access, get one. Web sites are inexpensive to create and maintain, and there are lots of companies and individuals who can design one for you. A web site isn't just an "extra." Today's savvy customers expect you to have an Internet presence. It sends a strong message about your agency's professionalism and gives them a 24/7 venue for transacting minor kinds of business directly with your agency. The more you turn technology to your benefit, the more you put your agency on a path of ever-increasing profitability.

So what's required to accomplish all of this? You'll need computer hardware, software, peripherals (printers, fax machine, scanner), and networking. If you're not comfortable determining what you need, hire a consultant. They're easy to find. A good place to start is the local community college. Additional referral sources are other agents in your area who have already made the technology leap. Be careful. Your needs depend on the mission of your agency. Keep that in mind when making any technology decisions.

Intuitively you might think there would be different technologies appropriate for different-sized agencies. That's not how it works, though. Fundamentally, every agency has the same technology needs. The only difference between small, medium, and large agencies is the number of pieces of equipment in an office. One rule applies: Everyone in the office dealing with customers should have a networked computer and phone at his or her desk and easy access to a printer, fax, and copier. Each computer should have the same software capabilities. Too many agencies upgrade computers one at a time. The new computers typically have different software than older versions. When that happens, employees can only operate their own computers. You want your staff—and you—to be able to function on every computer in the office.

Each person in your office should have e-mail. In larger agencies, inter-office communication can be significantly improved if staff can e-mail each other with questions and inquiries. In addition, everyone in the agency will have another way, besides the telephone, to communicate with customers. As I'll discuss later in this chapter, a segment of your customers would actually rather communicate with you via e-mail. In addition, e-mail can be a much cheaper and more efficient way to handle basic service work.

## What Your Computer System Needs to Do

Having extolled the virtues of technology, I offer an important caveat: Unless you're a sophisticated computer user, keep your system simple. You won't be doing yourself any favors if you buy sophisticated software that's so difficult to learn that no one uses it. You want your staff's learning curve short, and the staying power long. So stay focused on what you really need in order to run your agency effectively. Pay particular attention to technology that helps you build a strong customer database, a powerful electronic calendar system, and a flexible system for your back-room operations. Let's look at each in turn.

## CUSTOMER DATABASE

The customer is king, and the king's riches live in your database. To get to those riches, I recommend a database system from which you and your staff can swiftly and consistently retrieve your customer information. Again, you don't need to get fancy, but at the very least your database must allow you to input multiple ways to contact your customer. We're talking about the essentials such as each customer's home and business address, daytime phone number, cell phone number, pager number, fax number and e-mail address. Numerous ways to reach your customers can go a long way in blocking competitors, who may have no way to access clients beyond a nighttime home phone number.

You may find that of all the contact capabilities you include in your database, one of your strongest will be e-mail. In fact, if you don't have customer e-mail addresses in your database already, I recommend that you start capturing them right now. E-mail is increasingly a vital method of communication, especially with professional and business people. They don't have a lot of time and often prefer to handle their financial affairs, like insurance, by e-mail. Just like the fax machine, e-mail is now widely accepted as an important form of communication. Many office staffs find that using e-mail is terrific for quick follow-up notes, thank-you messages, and general marketing campaigns to build name recognition. They also use e-mail to efficiently communicate with underwriting, policy service personnel, and other company personnel. It's a great tool if you use it wisely. That means keeping your e-mails succinct. Nothing is more irritating than to receive a hundred e-mails in a day, only to discover that just two have any relevance to your business. And you always want your clients to view your e-mails as relevant.

Finally, you'll want your database to allow you to add the dates of significant events in your customers' lives—those milestones or anticipated transitions that let you provide a personal touch and identify cross-sell opportunities. Once your staff is up to speed on how best to get that information from your customers, you'll be surprised at how many such nuggets you'll want to add.

I'll talk about retooling your database to maximize its potential, including a method to capture e-mail addresses, in Chapter Eight.

# ELECTRONIC CALENDAR SYSTEM

Back in the olden days of insurance, a paper-based "tickler" system reminded us of appointments and when to do specific things. Today, all contact management systems have a calendar system that provides the same function, but much more easily and efficiently. Use it to your advantage because it can help you leverage the information that resides in your database.

Here's what your calendar system should do:

— View and print your schedule by day, week, or month;

— Set alarms to remind you of important customer events, such as X-dates;

— Schedule recurring events such as daily activities and weekly meetings;

— Avoid scheduling conflicts with automatic calendar notifications;

— Create date- and time-stamped notes for each customer contact to keep track of important conversations, commitments, and meeting notes;

— Track completed activities for each customer for a comprehensive record of meetings held, letters sent, e-mails sent and received, and calls completed.

The calendar will remind you when it's an appropriate, opportune time to contact your customer. In my agency, one of my staff members is designated as the "customer concierge." As the title suggests, the concierge is the primary person for increased customer contact, and in my office the role includes responsibility for making sure the database is continually updated. But even if you don't have a concierge—a position I'll talk more about later—every staff member needs access to this system in order to easily set, change, and reschedule appointments. Using an electronic calendar system also provides a more efficient method of keeping you and all agency producers fully booked with appointments for customer "face" time. Having the ability to track appointments is essential because it establishes accountability. Just by reviewing the calendar system, you can easily identify hard-working staff members and low producers.

But any good electronic calendar system goes well beyond just setting and tracking appointments. You need to incorporate a "hold file" or a "tickler" system for the following:

— Customer X-dates;

— Follow-up service issues;

— Your customers' life events such as birthdays, anniversaries, and retirement dates;

— Meetings involving office members, so that everyone always knows where someone is;

— Deadlines, such as production cut-off dates.

A good calendar system allows you to run a proactive agency. Instead of searching your desk every morning for files, an electronic calendar system defines your tasks on a daily basis. You're doing what you planned to do instead of reacting to what's in front of you.

## BACK-ROOM OPERATION

Somewhere in your agency, you've undoubtedly got people handling transactions by keying in applications, filling in forms, and doing whatever it takes to process the steady stream of information your agency generates. It's your back-room operation, and let's face it, to the untrained eye it may not seem terribly glamorous. But back-room operations are vital and need to be every bit as efficient as the rest of your agency's functions. How does technology help you do this? There's some debate. Certain proprietary systems help staff handle back-room operations in a seamless manner. Other proprietary systems don't do this part as well. My motto has always been, "Only worry about those things that you can control." You can easily control your database information and your electronic calendar system. You may not have as much control over your system for handling back-room operations. But you have more than one might think. If you understand the playing field and you know you're going to have problems with your carrier's proprietary system, then set up "work-arounds" to handle these situations. Go on the offensive and seize control rather than waiting for the perfect tool to come along. Technology is a tool that enables your agency to be more efficient and process work faster; it's not meant to do the job for you.

## Take the Leap: Go "File-less"

"Go paperless." It's the rallying cry of every tech salesman and company strategy "guru." Unfortunately, in our business it's simply impossible to go paperless altogether. Regulations require that we maintain certain paper documents, and some customers want everything on paper. But that doesn't mean you and your staff have to run to the file cabinets every time a customer calls with a question or change. That's what I mean by going "file-less": taking all the information that currently sits in your file cabinets and inputting it into your agency database. It's a more efficient way to operate. If you have a computer with customer information in it, you have all the tools to go "file-less." In fact, you're doing double the work if you use a computer database and still insist on maintaining paper files.

You might be anxious about this approach because it implies a riskier operating structure. It doesn't. In this day and age you always have to look for more efficient and productive ways to operate. Focus on the workflow and how you can do things differently. Going "file-less" is one of the steps to make your agency more productive and ultimately more profitable.

"But I have lots of files! It will take forever to input all the information in my files." This is a common objection I hear when I suggest that agents "go file-less." It's not an endless project, however, because you're only talking about data entry on the primary material that matters, such as customer names, relevant contact information, Social Security numbers—that sort of thing. The goal is to integrate the key data from paper into your database so that you have easy access and the ability to update electronically. Here are the steps I suggest:

1.  Divide your file cabinet into small pieces, either by letter or number of files.

2.  Set a target date for completion of this data entry task, making it no more than 120 days out. Go longer and your target date loses its sense of urgency.

3.  Determine how many files you need to input on a daily basis to reach your target completion date.

4.  Get to work.

Never miss a day of file inputting. Pick a specific time each day and schedule it for inputting. Aim for a time that's most optimal in your particular office. That may be the first hour in the day, or at lunch time, or at the close of your day. Whatever the hour, try to be consistent and most importantly, make sure the inputting doesn't fall behind. In my experience, you need this kind of discipline to get the job finished.

## FROM TRIAL AND ERROR TO TRULY FILE-LESS

*Years ago I knew that moving to a file-less system was the way to go, but the people on my staff actually responsible for the day-to-day processing of paperwork felt it would be tough not to work with something tangible. They thought it would be too daunting, too overwhelming. I understood their concerns, so at first we tried to phase it in. That actually created a bigger mess because we wound up serving two masters instead of taking the leap. So one day I decided to just box up the files, take them off-site to the dustiest, dirtiest warehouse I could find. That way, the files were still available, but nobody wanted to go get them. From that point on we had a cut-off date, which made it easier to do things on a go-forward basis. Everything new went to a file assistant. If you needed something prior to the cut-off date, you knew where the files were and you'd have to get them.*

*Bam! Everyone moved to the file-less system immediately.*

*Given an option, human beings go to the easiest fall-back position. Since then, I've trained thousands of agents how to go file-less and I've come up with better methods of breaking it down and not moving everything all in one day. But for me at the time, taking the plunge flat-out meant cutting the cord. And now? I can't even imagine going back to paper files.*

If you're just starting your career, go "file-less" the day you begin. Although you'd obviously need to have the technology to support it from the get-go, the cost isn't that significant when compared to the benefits.

## Working File-Less on an Everyday Basis

Let's assume that you've inputted all your existing files into a database filled with all the customer information you've collected in your agency. How do you change your workflow to maximize your technology every day? Here's what I recommend. Applications and changes, when signed, go to the agent or office director who checks that the applications and changes were entered and issued correctly. The date of policy issue or change is entered into the agency computer system. Paperwork is then sent to a scanning station. This station can be at the receptionist's or a data entry specialist's desk. There the documents are scanned into a folder labeled by month and year. Just make sure that you check in advance with your state Department of Insurance to make sure that your scanning procedures comply with relevant regulations. Regulations are in place to ensure that electronic versions of paper documents retain their legal status, and those regulations can vary by state. But assuming you've done that, and after the scanning process is complete—brace yourself now—the paper-work itself is then shredded.

I know you may be shuddering at the thought, but don't worry. The computer at the scanning station is backed up to a tape drive every night, and the tape is stored in a fireproof safe. Scanning documents and using electronic storage eliminate the need for most of your file cabinets. Follow up by networking your scanning station to your inter-office computer system. Networking allows your staff to access scanned documents in real time when talking to a customer. That's an enormous advantage, but if the prospect still makes the hairs on your arms stand straight up, don't forget that anything you've scanned can always be printed later. You're not throwing out the information. You're only storing it differently—and much more efficiently.

In my experience the cost for a file-less system with scanning is approximately $1,000-$2,500. If that sounds too rich for your blood, check the prices on file cabinets. Consider that a single four-drawer metal file cabinet with locks will likely run you at least $200. We're talking about the plain Jane version, which obviously doesn't come with protective fire-coating. Now factor in how many file cabinets you'd need as your business grows, the floor space those cabinets suck out of the square footage in your office, and the file folders you'll blaze through. Never mind the maintenance file cabinets require. Just look at the cost. See it mounting? Go file-less, however, and in addition to getting rid of those clunky cabinets, you'll also eliminate the need for a part-time employee to do nothing but file. You can reassign that person to do more productive work, such as data entry.

## Proprietary Versus "Off-the-Shelf" Systems

My research and work with agents nationwide has shown that there is no uniformity in the insurance industry when it comes to the use of database technology. Therefore, I don't advocate one database system over another. But the first thing an agent needs to understand is that a database system can't effectively serve two masters. Captive agents tend to use their company's proprietary system, plus a parallel system such as GoldMine, ACT! or one of several others available. It's the same for independent agencies, except they might have to use several proprietary systems required by their carriers. Where things can get gnarly is when agents use the proprietary system for back-room support and the "off-the-shelf" software for customer relationship management. Those off-the-shelf systems might have a more friendly "point and click" approach, but I'm convinced that using a dual-system approach is wrong. As soon as you get involved with multiple systems you have to cope with the labor costs in maintaining them and endure the painstaking challenge of keeping everything synchronized. That's not how you want to be spending your time or your staff resources.

Let's weigh the cost of parallel systems against what you might lose if you only use one system. In my experience, very little was lost. That's because even if some proprietary systems are more awkward to use, as long as you have the ability to input critical information there's really no reason to buy a supplementary system. What you want are the essentials: the ability to log incoming or outgoing calls with detailed notes; the capability to send correspondence and mass solicitations; a ready way to keep a household profile that includes names, addresses, phone numbers, other ways to contact, dates of birth, occupations, and so on. You'll also want a section to note customer likes, dislikes, and policy information on every line of insurance—whether placed with your agency or not. Some systems score high marks for doing all of that. Some are weaker. But what little you might have to forfeit by sticking with just one database is easily justified against the burden of supporting two parallel database systems.

Remember, that for every action there is an equal and opposite reaction. In context of our insurance agency world, it means that gaining some real cool stuff in a second system can lead to a lot of unnecessary work on a consistent basis.

# Take Measure of Your Technology Purchases

The critical mistake people make with technology is declaring victory when they buy new hardware or software instead of measuring their effectiveness once they are installed. If you've evaluated your needs correctly and avoided buying technology that you don't need, you'll probably be in good shape. But even then, you'll want to know just how much bang you're getting for your buck, and to do that you need to establish benchmarks to measure your technology's effectiveness.

I've developed a simple approach for evaluating the time and money spent on new technology. If you know you're going to upgrade or change the way you use technology, wait four full weeks before implementing the changes. During those four weeks, measure total sales per week, incoming calls per week, outgoing service and sales calls per week, and cross-sales resulting from both incoming and outgoing sales calls. Factor in the seasonality of your four-week period. (Is it typically a high, average, or slow time of the year for your agency?) Then take the average for all the metrics described above. Once you start using your new technology calculate the same metrics 90 days after you implement the technology, again for a four-week period that as much as possible takes into account your original parameters of seasonality and so forth. The process will allow you to train your staff and work out the bugs. You should see a significant improvement. Establish a payback period and continue to measure your agency's productivity every week. Do this for a 12-month period. That's my method for making sure I know that the technology I implemented paid off.

# Upgrading and Maintaining Technology

How do you know when to upgrade? Technology continues to change so quickly that your office systems are probably out of date. That doesn't mean you have to replace them. You don't want to be the first on the block to buy new hardware or software. Use some healthy skepticism, and view technology in the same way you would when considering a new model-year automobile. You'd most likely want to wait until the second model year before you buy it, giving the automaker time to correct any kinks that surfaced in the vehicle's inaugural year.

On the other hand, our industry is intensely competitive, so don't make the mistake of being the last on the block to invest in genuinely valuable improvements. Make a point of developing different technology information resources, from magazines to other agents who are technology savvy. Once you learn that an agent is installing some hardware or software that you're interested in, telephone him. Tell him that you're considering the same hardware or software, and ask if you can come by his office to see how it's working. Most people will invite you over. After all, they're proud of their purchase and want to show it off. Ask lots of questions, especially of the staff, to gauge how easy it will be to integrate the system into your agency. That way, you'll gather valuable information that will enable you to make an informed decision on whether to upgrade to that system or not.

Of course, even when you're satisfied that you've got the technology you need to operate your agency at peak efficiency, don't take that as a license to forget about it for the next five years. No matter how well your business seems to be running, it's often what you don't see that can hurt you. Think of it as you might a tire with a slow leak. As long as your car is faithfully getting you from Point A to Point B, you're probably clueless that there's a problem. All along, though, your tire has steadily been losing pressure and one day, it's just "suddenly" flat. There you are, stuck in the driveway while your competitors are cruising the interstate. The same is true with technology. If you don't keep an eye on your agency's information systems—whether they're hardware or software systems—one day you'll discover that they're failing you. It's a jolt, and worse, the investment you face to bring those systems back up to speed is probably nowhere in your budget. Your best bet? Anticipate and evaluate. In fact, make technology part of your ongoing budget process. Evaluate it at least once a year and allocate accordingly.

Bottom line: It's not the technology that's important, it's how you use it to boost your agency's efficiency. If you want your office to run more smoothly, then commit to make today's technology work for you.

Now that you have assembled the pieces necessary to take your business to a new level, in the next chapter I'll talk about different structures for your agency and take a new look at marketing. There is gold to be had if you know where to look.

# Chapter Highlights

— You need technology to keep up, but assess your needs carefully. Everything you buy or upgrade must perform in a way that provides ever-improving service for your customers and better cross-sell opportunities for you.

— Minimal technology tools include computers on every desk, compatible software in each, networking and e-mail capabilities, high-speed Internet access, a web site, and sufficient peripherals.

— Don't get seduced by bells and whistles. Overly sophisticated technology won't do you any good if no one has the time or patience to learn it.

— No matter what technology you integrate into your office, make sure that together they include a powerful customer database, a robust electronic calendar accessible to every staff member, and a flexible system for back-room operations.

— Ditch your file cabinets and go file-less. Input existing paperwork into your database and scan subsequent entries into your system. Back it all up daily. You're not losing anything. You're merely storing it more efficiently.

— To the degree possible, avoid using more than one database. You'll save yourself the headache of making double entries and keeping everything synchronized.

— Once you've purchased new technology, make sure you got what you paid for by evaluating its effectiveness over a 12-month period.

— Don't get caught in a never-ending upgrade cycle, but do evaluate your technology needs annually, and budget for them accordingly.

PROFIT FROM CHANGE

# PART THREE

# RETOOLING YOUR AGENCY

PROFIT FROM CHANGE

# RETOOLING
# YOUR STAFF

CHAPTER SEVEN

$N$ow that you see the opportunities in front of you and have taken a closer look at what you do in your agency, I want to show you how to streamline your agency to achieve the greatest impact. You have learned that there will be a positive return if you manage each line of insurance and each employee as a profit center. But how do you actually reposition your agency? Well, remember the old Chinese proverb that says the journey of a thousand miles begins with a single step? For you, the journey is to boldly move your agency into the future. And that step? You've already taken one just by reading this book and rethinking your focus. Now it's time to put another foot forward. I'm going to show you how to march ahead by redefining your agency's structure, and retooling your staff in a way that helps everyone in your office not just meet your expectations, but exceed them.

## HOW IT ALL STARTED

*While driving by a large factory one day I noticed people moving old equipment out of one of its buildings and moving new equipment in. It was obvious what was occurring. The manufacturing plant was taking out an old production line and replacing it with a new production line in order to manufacture*

*whatever widget the owners wanted to produce. This is a*
*common occurrence in manufacturing. The owners had shut*
*down their production line in order to retool their manufactur-*
*ing company for the future. It struck me that this manufacturing*
*business must have calculated that the cost/benefit of closing*
*down its factory to retool was an essential investment to*
*increase efficiencies and boost revenues.*

# Two Types of Agencies

Before you can retool, you have to know what needs to be fixed.
Many of today's agencies operate as generalist agencies. In order
to capitalize on today's changes they need to become specialist
agencies.

## THE OLD MODEL—THE GENERALIST AGENCY

Most of us defaulted to building our agencies using a generalist
approach, which for years was the prevailing business model in
our industry. As generalists, we hired employees to assist us in all
lines of insurance. It worked in the past because we typically only
serviced one, two, or possibly three lines of insurance.

Then companies introduced more products, but also maintained
pressure to continue levels of production in all lines. Most
agencies (yours included, I imagine) became overwhelmed and

helpless to integrate these additional products and services, even though it was understood that customers desired them. For you it might have gone something like this: There was the introduction of the umbrella, then the transition from auto and fire to an auto, fire, and commercial agency. Then you were asked to offer life, health, disability, and long-term care insurance. As your agency and staff grew you continued to hire employees with a generalist attitude and mindset. That is, when you hired new employees you taught them the process for each line of insurance so they could provide all services to all customers. Each member of your staff was trying to be all things to all people.

In recent years, however, the generalist model has fallen into disfavor because its "one size fits all" mentality too often cripples agency growth. Why? It takes too long to train people on multiple products, especially if a new hire has no background in insurance. Think back to your own early days in the business. You didn't know how you would master all of the things you needed to know. Remember how overwhelmed you felt? It's no different today for a new employee you hire.

But there's another reason the generalist model has cracked under the strain of changes in our industry: accountability. The generalist model makes it too hard to get a fix on how much benefit employees provide. As generalists, their role is so broad you can't

accurately quantify their contribution. If you could you'd probably be disappointed, anyway. That's because if you give someone
a hundred things to do he'll never be great at any one of them.
But if you give that person one thing to do, he can master that
activity and ultimately excel at it.

## THE WINNING MODEL—THE SPECIALIST AGENCY

Happily, there's a way out of the generalist mess. It's the specialist model, and if you're serious about growing your business and
properly serving your customers, you need to transition to it.
Under the specialist model, all of your employees—present and
future—develop expertise in one specific area. You'd have, for
instance, a life-only specialist, an auto-only specialist, a health-
only specialist, and so on.

Here's how a typical specialist agency looks:

| | | |
|---|---|---|
| Auto Department<br>CSR<br>Account Executive | Fire Department<br>CSR<br>Account Executive | Commercial<br>Department<br>CSR<br>Account Executive |
| Life Department<br>CSR<br>Account Executive | Financial Services<br>Department<br>CSR<br>Account Executive | Health/Long-Term<br>Care Department<br>CSR<br>Account Executive |

In the specialist model, employees have a shorter learning curve because they only have one product or area to master. It's quick and easy to learn direct input into the computer for one product line. It's less demanding to learn one set of underwriting rules compared to learning many. And, as staff members master their respective areas of responsibility, they gain a strong sense of self worth and value, instead of feeling as if they're treading water.

Finally, the specialist model allows you to evaluate whether any given employee is a profit center, because each has a well-defined job description and guidelines for accountability. In turn, that makes it easier to quantify when an additional employee is needed—bearing in mind, of course, that your existing employees have to be profit centers before you add any new staff.

In the end, using the specialist model is win-win for your staff, and certainly one for you in developing profit centers. Integrate it into your agency and watch what happens. I'm betting it won't take long for you to celebrate the difference between sluggish, incremental growth (or even no growth) and what I call quantum-leap growth. Go for it!

## Focus, Focus, Focus

An important component of the specialist model is to create synergy and focus to meet the overall goals and objectives of the agency. It's important that you build a team of people who can assist you in "working the system" and that you delegate responsibility and accountability in this area. The benefit? You're no longer dependent on one superstar employee.

## YOUR CALENDAR PROGRAM AND ACCOUNTABILITY

*One of the best ways I've found to keep people accountable and focused is by using the calendar system to post your daily goals, the daily contacts you need to make, and more importantly, your daily review of what you're trying to accomplish. If you're trying to set appointments, then your calendar needs to give you "pop-up" reminders. If your focus is to have a regularly scheduled staff meeting, then you'd want to calendar each meeting at least a day in advance to remind everyone to be in attendance.*

By now you may be wondering how you'd go about cross-selling products if you have specialists focused on just one area. Well, even though your employees specialize in one product line, they need to know enough about each other's products to incorporate them into discussions with customers. That's not the same as using a generalist approach, because product familiarization is different than product expertise. Thus, your goal is to have your employees conversant enough about products outside their specialty so that when they grab the phone they don't miss an opportunity to talk to a customer about a product or service that isn't already in that customer's household. But once they've seized an opportunity, the appropriate specialist can follow through on the fine points where expertise is truly required. It's carefully orchestrated teamwork in your office, but it's seamless for your customer.

For any system to work effectively, you have to use it every day. It's the follow-through that spells success for any agency that wants to expand into the future. Remember, your primary focus—serving the needs of your customers—is the whole reason to develop an efficient system of customer contact and customer follow-up.

## The Transformation Process

I'll say it again: Your staff is the foundation of your agency. Therefore, it's absolutely essential that everyone you employ understands and embraces your vision for the agency. It's a building-block process, and one you'll be glad you undertook. Read on to learn about the simple building blocks that will make it work.

### BUILDING BLOCK 1:
### GET YOUR STAFF TO BUY INTO YOUR VISION

Sit down with your staff to discuss your vision for the future. Talk to them about your plans to convert from a generalist to a specialist agency, and why it would be more effective and comfortable for everyone. Then, whether you have one, two, or more staff members when you decide to transition to the "specialist" model, ask them to list their current duties. By writing their job functions out, preferably on a white board or on a yellow pad, you'll see that they have many responsibilities. Some examples? Taking in information to quote auto, quoting the auto, processing the application, inspections, and so forth. With fire insurance, their lists likely would include taking in mortgagee information, quote information, quoting fire, processing the applications, arranging for inspections, etc. It's essentially the same process for life, commercial, long-term care, and health insurance.

Once the list with your staff members' job duties is compiled, it becomes obvious that their days are regularly consumed by many and varied responsibilities. Ask them this: "If you could get rid of one thing during the day to help you become more efficient, what would it be?" You might find, for example, that you've got a clerk who doesn't enjoy processing life applications or doesn't care for the pressure of handling numerous auto customers. If one of those aspects of responsibility was removed from her "generalist plate," then she would be able to be more effective in other areas.

By completing this exercise your staff members will see that by taking on a specialist role they'll actually have more control of their workday and will be more effective. Stress that the transition won't happen overnight. It will be an ongoing process, but one that ultimately will allow them to remove responsibilities from their plates that don't directly relate to their areas of specialization. Impress on them that moving forward as a specialist agency will give them the opportunity to focus on what they enjoy. And as everyone will tell you, a happy employee is a productive employee. That translates into success in the future.

Will all staff members embrace your new vision? Most will, but a few might not. After all, as you move through the process of evaluating existing positions and identifying staff members' strengths and weaknesses, it'll become increasingly apparent which person you want to specialize in any given area. Even though you will have involved your staff in that process, not everyone is comfortable with change. Some may not be pleased with specializing in one area. There may be valid reasons for how they feel: insecurity, losing a perceived power base, or just not being the type who will fit into your new model. That's okay. Those people, even though they may have been good employees, still might balk at moving forward with you. You might have to make the hard decision to let them go. If that's the case, so be it. You can't let your business rely on one or two people. It has to rely on effectively using the systems you put into place.

Of course, it's possible that you'll have one employee who doesn't precisely fit into the specialist model but who totally understands and enthusiastically embraces what you're trying to accomplish. Keep in the back of your mind that this person could be your office director, your chief of staff, your main lieutenant for carrying out the tactical plan you've instituted. But a word of caution is in order. Before putting someone in that very important position, make sure he or she possesses the necessary skills, and has the ability to manage and inspire people. If you don't, you might be creating a position that can inadvertently backfire on you.

## BUILDING BLOCK 2:
## FILLING THE GAPS

After assigning your staff members to their new roles, you may have gaps or positions that aren't covered. To fulfill your vision, you'll need to hire additional staff. Hire a customer service representative first. You want your staff to do more "people work" than paperwork. If you hire a producer first, you're essentially creating a lot of paperwork with no back-office infrastructure.

You'll want your CSR to be a profit center just like everyone else, however. Help your new hire hit the ground running by teaching him or her how to recognize sales opportunities in conversations with customers. You want every CSR trained to be proactive by being information gatherers and information givers.

## WILL YOU HAVE A SIDE SALAD
## WITH YOUR PIZZA?

*I was informed by my son Michael and my daughter Emily that it was my turn to cook dinner one evening. I told them that "it would be no problem," so I hung up and I phoned Pizza Hut and ordered a large pizza to go. When I stopped in to pick it up, the clerk at the counter courteously greeted me and said, "Mr. Korsgaden, I see that you like jalapeno peppers and ranch dressing. Would you like that on your side salads?" Well, I hadn't ordered side salads, but it seemed like a good idea so I said, "Sure." Then the counter girl said, "I also see that your family usually has Pepsi with your pizza. Would you like a six-pack to go?" And I replied, "Yes."*

*All the information was in Pizza Hut's database. The counter girl brought up my preferences and up-sold me on side salads and soft drinks when all I had ordered was a pizza.*

Once your CSR is successful, graduate the person to an account executive/producer position. Then hire the next CSR and repeat the process all over again. Depending on the size of your agency you may want to include an office manager to oversee day-to-day operations, thereby freeing up your time to do what you do best—meeting with customers and keeping a full calendar of sales appointments.

I know that building a customer-focused specialist agency takes time. In fact, it may take several years. But if you include it in your road map and keep at it one step at a time, it'll happen. Simply start by building one department to be a profit center, then go on to building the next department, and so on. You'll get there.

# Chapter Highlights

— The generalist approach for agency organization worked fine when you were selling only one or two product lines. But to see growth in today's multiple-product agencies, transition to the winning model—the specialist agency.

— Specialist agencies make it possible to measure the productivity and effectiveness of each staff member—and keep everyone focused on being profit centers.

— Retooling your agency with a specialist model demands that you concentrate on meeting your new goals and creating synergy among your staff. Get employees to buy into your vision by involving them in the process from the start.

— Although the specialist model calls for employees to develop expertise in specific product lines, make sure they still have a working knowledge of products outside their areas. Everyone needs to know enough to recognize cross-sell opportunities when customers call.

— To fill any gaps not covered by a specialist role, hire a CSR. But make sure your CSR is also a profit center!

PROFIT FROM CHANGE

# RETOOLING YOUR DATABASE

## CHAPTER | EIGHT

Now that your retooling process is under way, you need to leverage one of your most important assets—customer information in your database. It's an underused tool in a generalist agency. But assuming that you've freed up your staff members to focus on specific areas, it's natural for them to want more information about your customers. In this chapter, you'll learn the steps to retool and update your database, and discover a wealth of sales opportunities—all while building closer relationships with your customers.

## Setting the Stage for Your Database Retooling Day

Fasten your seatbelts, because here's what you need to do to retool your database: You need to shut down your agency for a customer-calling campaign unlike anything you've ever done before. Yes, you read that last sentence correctly, but believe me when I tell you that the world will not come to an end. Tell your staff well in advance what you're going to do. Fire them up; let them know that they're going to surprise your customers in a positive way. Pick the day of the week that's quietest, probably not a Monday or Tuesday.

I'll discuss this in more detail shortly, but briefly, your mission on retooling day will be to get each member of your staff on the phone to call every one of your customers. Your staff's objective isn't to make sales—although that may happen as a by-product. Rather, their goal is to simply thank each customer for his or her business and bolster your agency's database with new or updated information.

Your staff will simply begin each call with this:

> *"Thank you for being our customer. We really appreciate your business."*

In my experience, customers have always been pleasantly surprised and happy to receive special attention and appreciation. The power of those two little words—"thank you"—is awesome!

But it's the second part of what your staff says to customers that's critical to the agency. Specifically:

> *"We're calling to update our records and to make sure we have all the information we need to serve you the best way possible."*

## DATABASE RETOOLING DAY

*In modeling my business after the factory I had observed*

*retooling its equipment, I created a plan in which I shut down my agency for one whole day to "retool" for the future. Why the database first? Well, though I'd always insisted that "the one with the most information wins," I wasn't practicing what I preached. So first I identified the products that our agency offers, then scripted a plan of attack to call each of our current customers and investigate which of these products they needed and that they didn't have with my agency.*

*You're probably thinking, "Wow! That's a tall order!" It's not. It's very achievable. We had several goals: reconnect with our customers, gather information, and deepen our relationship with them. We needed to pinpoint exactly what policies they had—whether with us or another company—and learn what was going on in their lives so that we could better help them. And we did this not with a sales call, but with a helpful, person-to-person "thank-you" call.*

*The first step was to have everyone in the agency clear their calendars on that day. Next we arranged to forward all incoming calls to our answering service. We gave the answering service a script:*

**The Korsgaden Agency is closed today to conduct a special customer survey that will allow us to serve you better. If this is an emergency, please call [cell number]. For claims call [800 number]. Regular office hours will**

**resume [day and date], so leave a message and we'll call you back. Thank you and have a great day.**

*Of course, since we're in the service business we set up a cell phone for calls concerning claims, emergencies, and other "can't wait" possibilities, and assigned one person to man that phone.*

*Some staff members regarded the plan with major hesitation. They wondered how clients would react when they learned we were closed on a business day. They also wondered whether clients would view our calls as an intrusion. But I reminded everyone that our first goal was to thank customers, and the second to ask for household information that would allow us to serve them even better.*

So how do you prepare to update your customers' information? Use the Household Update Sheet **(Appendix Two)** as a guide to develop a form that lists all the products your agency currently offers. You need to be very specific here. For example, do you offer automobile insurance on traditional cars that are driven on a day-to-day basis, and also insurance on classic cars, motorcycles, boats, jet skis, or yachts? Do you additionally offer auto warranty insurance? Can your agency handle an auto loan? If so, do you also offer credit life insurance? Include anything and everything that might relate to fulfilling somebody's, as we say, "auto protection needs." Try to get as specific as you can for each line of business that you currently offer, and include it on your Household Update Sheet. Then make copies and distribute them to every person who will be making calls.

## Retooling Day Has Arrived!

This should be a fun day, so treat it as such. Decorate your office with streamers and balloons. Arrange for lunch to be delivered to the office. Have some cash on hand for "spot bonuses" to staff members if they gain information on a pre-determined number of customers. As a gesture to show appreciation, also plan to reward all staff members with a gift such as dinner for two, theater tickets, or gift certificates. You'll see immediately how quickly your employees get into the spirit of the day. The whole office atmosphere will be different.

Tell your staff that retooling the database is just one small part of the retooling process. Appoint someone, possibly yourself, to be both cheerleader and coach. Set up a "command central" to ensure that all client requests for information are processed on the spot. Divide the client list between staff members. Get everyone in on the action. Your receptionist, your CSRs, your account executives, your claims handler—everybody needs to be on the phone making outbound customer calls! If you have a district manager, recruit him or her to help out. Everyone who works in the agency needs to understand the mission and pitch in. It's amazing what can happen in any agency if the strategy is fueled with enthusiasm. Dial with a smile, it's contagious!

## IMMEDIATE OBJECTIVES

Once you have a plan of attack in place and everyone is fired up, you're ready to start working the phones. The calls aren't hard to make, but that doesn't mean you don't have specific goals. Here they are:

1. First, tell each customer, "Thank you for doing business with our agency."

2. Second, answer any questions customers have about products already placed with your agency.

3. Third, update your database on each household, noting detailed information on different opportunities to contact each client. Key information to get or update includes e-mail addresses, pager, cell and fax numbers, and so on.

Ask for X-dates on policies that aren't placed with your agency, and be sure to note potential sales opportunities. For example, let's say that during a call you discover that one of your customers has a three-year car loan that he's just about to pay off.

That little nugget should trigger upcoming sales opportunities because your customer might be interested in purchasing a new car and securing a new car loan. Another possibility triggered by the end of a three-year car loan is the likelihood that your customer's factory warranty is about to expire. The client may be in the market for auto warranty insurance. You want to know when he purchased the car, and then you can identify a likely sales event. Ask questions such as, "When did you purchase your home?" This question identifies yet another sales event. If the home is covered with home warranty insurance, every year it renews at the same time. By learning the date you create an opportunity for a sale of home warranty coverage. If flood insurance is important in your market, be sure to zero in on which carrier currently covers that and when the policy expires, which offers another sales event.

Ask your customers if they want a personal review of their policies. Offering a policy review gives you the opportunity to let them know what new products and additional services are available through your agency. Perhaps you now offer banking services and/or investment products. You can't assume your customers know or remember that you offer these services, even though you may have sent a letter or two announcing them. Share details about the new products you offer, such as checking accounts, CDs, and other banking products. The conversation opens doors to a discussion of your ability to help in the financial services arena and how you can assist them in asset accumulation. As you can see, the opportunities for add-on business are substantial.

## STAY ALERT FOR UNEXPECTED SALES OPPORTUNITIES

Although your immediate aim on retooling day is to update household information, you may well be pleasantly surprised by unexpected sales opportunities. Be ready for them! While your staff members are working the phones, for example, they may turn up some customers who spontaneously raise issues relating to existing products or other products they have. Those unexpected questions have actual and immediate sales potential, and you'll obviously want to handle them without delay. In still other instances, the information you obtain will prompt specific questions or other potential product sale opportunities. For example, say you have a customer named Mrs. Emerson and during a retooling call you learn that her work number recently changed. Was the change due to a promotion within her existing company? Or did she take a new job? Is the new job far enough away that she might move? What about a 401(k) account with her previous employer? Did she have one and would she like to roll it over?

Here's another example. You've got a customer named Mr. Rojas.

He's an auto-only client, but you just learned that he has a new home address. That should mean to you that Mr. Rojas might have either purchased a home or is renting in a new location. The information opens the door to homeowners insurance or a renter's policy. That's the kind of potential you don't want to miss, so be prepared for anything on your retooling day. Get what you need. But get more if you can.

## GETTING THROUGH

Depending upon the size of your agency, getting through to all of your customers might take just one day or it might take longer. In larger agencies, and this was our experience, we didn't get through our entire customer base in one day, even with everyone on staff making calls. In fact, we predict that you'll actually contact fewer than 25 percent of your clients on the first day. Some won't answer the phone. You'll find that you have an old phone number for others. And, not surprisingly, for still others you'll only be able to leave a message. As a result, you'll need to run additional retooling days, about a month apart, until all customers have been contacted. Of course, wherever you're in the retooling process, stress to everyone how important it is to set up appointments with customers at every opportunity. Your goal is to have an actual dialogue with each of your customers in order to ask specific questions about every household.

Don't be daunted by the database retooling task. Not only will it bring you much closer to your overall objective to connect with your customers in a meaningful way, but a retooled database will make your life easier on a day-by-day basis. After all, your staff will have an already-established system in place from which to capture customer information on a daily basis. More on that in a moment.

## FOLLOWING THROUGH

The "thank you" call is the beginning of a different kind of dialogue with your customers. That dialogue shouldn't be isolated to your retooling day, and it shouldn't end once you've talked with all your customers. Of paramount importance is the follow-through process. When a customer expresses an interest in a particular product, send out the information that day. Then immediately schedule a follow-up call within seven days. It's all about timing and opportunity.

# Everyday Retooling

After retooling day, it struck me and my staff that although we did a great job of making calls to contact customers and set appointments, we didn't do as well in seeking information on incoming calls. For instance, if a customer called in to make a car change or had a question on a claim, our CSRs handled the transaction or answered the customer's questions, but failed to deepen the relationship by updating pertinent household information. We soon recognized that we were so busy doing the servicing that we didn't properly pivot to other product lines during these calls, although we had every intention of doing so.

What happened to us wasn't unique. Many agents complain that they're so inundated with incoming calls that they can't get to the business at hand—making sales. But what we recognized—as you will—is that those calls aren't interruptions at all. They're opportunities to forge ever-deeper relationships with customers, and to gain and share information. Frankly, to treat those calls with nonchalance is a luxury none of us can afford. Our industry is too intense and competitive for passive thinking.

In my agency, recognition of the problem gave birth to new resolve, and then a solution. We moved aggressively to leverage incoming calls by creating a new position in the agency—the customer concierge. I briefly mentioned the position in Chapter 6, and you may recall that it's the concierge who's responsible for taking the lead in making absolutely sure I stay in touch with my customers. To meet that role, the concierge assists in completing database information and providing increased customer contact. Here's how it works: After every incoming call, the CSR enters into the computer his or her notes regarding the contact. At 7:00

every evening the computer spits out the names of those customers and the reasons for their calls. Some days the list is two pages long. On other days the list runs to 20 pages. No matter what the reason for the call, a notation is made so that the customer concierge can call the customer just to make certain that everything was taken care of satisfactorily. It's a powerful way to cement relationships with clients. They know we're there. They know we care.

## EVEN THE FORD DEALER HAS A CUSTOMER CONCIERGE

*A friend of ours relayed the following experience. She phoned the local Ford dealership to get an additional key made for her Lincoln Town Car. The service manager told her they couldn't fulfill her request because they didn't carry that key in stock. Usually that would have been the end of the story. Not in this case. The next day the auto dealer's customer concierge phoned and asked, "I see you called the dealership yesterday. Was everything handled to your satisfaction?" Our friend replied, "No, you guys don't carry Lincoln keys in stock." The concierge then gave her the name, address, and directions to the nearest Lincoln dealer. She was so impressed with the special treatment and follow-up that she's told her friends about the experience.*

Do those incoming calls really matter that much? Yes! In fact, no matter how minor the information from a call might seem, you need to view that nugget as if it were the Holy Grail. Immediately provide those callers with information on products and services that you know they need based on whatever little sliver of information they gave you. By retooling your database you built yourself a beautifully engineered bridge to the high-quality and high-density households you need to grow your agency. Keep it maintained. Take advantage of every call that comes in.

## What You Will Discover

I've helped thousands of agencies go through the retooling process. The volume and depth of information they obtained exceeded their wildest expectations and I'm absolutely convinced that the same will happen in your agency.

You'll uncover lots of new ways to contact your customers and capture information. And talk about instant gratification—you'll discover many "hot leads." A hot lead is someone who is interested in receiving product information right now and has a high probability of an immediate purchase. You'll also receive many "warm" leads from people who are receptive to talking with you about additional products in the near future. Be sure to capture this information in your database. You can use it as internal X-dates for future follow-up.

My own experience showed me that the best opportunities for additional sales were in the area of umbrella policies, life insurance, and investment products. Each customer has different needs, but one thing became clear to me: My staff and I didn't know our customers as well as I thought we did. For example, the amount of investment assets our customers held was unbelievable. Another surprise: People have money stashed away in 401(k)s, T-bills, CDs and so on. It was remarkable! It soon became obvious that we had hit a home run. Looking back it was more like a grand slam!

## It's a Numbers Game

The information in your database opens the door to launch a direct-mail campaign to share information with your customers or prospects. It's a numbers game. Share enough information with enough people and sales will result. But after you've sent a letter and made a follow-up phone call to ask for an appointment, then what? Your philosophy should be that your agency is offering a product or service that your clients should consider for their family. Thus, you need to take one more step by putting into your electronic calendar what the next focus is going to be for each household. The focus might be auto, it might be life, but don't put away your electronic file until you've defined that next call, that "next step," and scheduled it for follow-up.

That's why an up-to-date database is so important. Once you put information in the system, you need "touch points" to make sure you stay in front of the client and keep his interest level high so that you can make the conversion from a prospect to an actual new policy sold in the household.

## IN THE OLD DAYS OF RUNNING MY AGENCY...

*Let's say I had a client named Mr. Jones. I would go out to see him and write an auto insurance policy. I would say, "We offer homeowners, too. We give a discount when you have both your auto and home insured with our company." Mr. Jones would typically say, "Great! I would really be interested in that when the policy comes up for renewal." Mr. Jones was motivated because he had just purchased a product from me— the trust and the connection was there. I would write the date on an X-date card, and note, "Don't forget to call Mr. Jones regarding homeowners insurance." Invariably I would file the card, then something would always come up that would deter me from calling him to get that follow-up sale.*

*What a stupid way for me to try to build my business. Sure, I usually had a good excuse. I was busy writing new business on other clients or maybe I was overloaded with paperwork. But for whatever reason I overlooked that extra potential sale. Worse yet, by the time I finally did get around to calling Mr.*

*Jones, the X-date had come and gone and I had lost his trust because I didn't deliver on my promise to follow through. Is it any wonder that Mr. Jones's enthusiasm was gone and my credibility with him was lost?*

The database should drive you to action. Automate it so that it tells you every day the things that you need to do. It should create a complete "to do" list that won't go away until you have checked each item off in the computer as being done. As you complete each item, mark on your calendar when the next step should occur. For example: During a conversation with Mrs. Emily Stowe you discover that she will soon inherit some money from her late parents' estate. Your calendar item should read: "Set appointment with Mrs. Emily Stowe to discuss investing inheritance." Set the date and the notation will automatically come up on your "to do" list on that day. If you use your electronic calendar program and database consistently, I promise you'll wonder how you ever did without them in the past.

# Chapter Highlights

— Manufacturing companies regularly shut down their production lines to retool for the newest model of whatever widget they're manufacturing. It works for them, so why shouldn't the concept work for an insurance/financial services agency? It does!

— Do some "staging" for your staff so everyone gets caught up in the importance and excitement of Database Retooling Day. Have some fun with it and watch the enthusiasm build.

— I'm always preaching, "Build closer relationships with your customers." By scheduling a retooling day and saying "thank you," you're putting that philosophy into action.

— It isn't enough to touch base with your customers on retooling day. Capitalize on those calls with immediate and tenacious follow-up!

— Don't look at incoming calls as an interference. They're opportunities. Seize them!

— Let your retooled database help you with scheduling by making use of "pop-up" reminders for appointments and important "touch points" with customers.

— Agencies that have been through the retooling process are reaping the rewards—closer ties with their customers, additional sales opportunities, and filling unmet customer needs.

PROFIT FROM CHANGE

# RETOOLING YOUR CUSTOMER RELATIONSHIPS

CHAPTER | NINE

Once you've retooled your database information and discovered the wealth of potential within your own agency, how do you keep the momentum going? You put a system into place to ensure that your database continues to grow and expand. Think of your database as a lake fed by a mountain stream; it needs fresh water coming into it, or eventually it will stagnate and dry up. That fresh water is your customer base. Your customers change jobs, cars, the loans on their cars. They get married, divorced, have children. By now, none of this is news to you, but to capture all those timely changes and capitalize on them you need a procedure that carries you well beyond Database Retooling Day. It just so happens I have one for you. It's called the Relationship-Focused Agency (RFA) System.

## Relationship-Focused Agency System

The RFA System will help you redefine how you conduct the business of your agency on a going-forward basis. Instead of reacting in a defensive mode all day, the RFA System enables you to take the offensive and control what's happening. It works by helping you segment your customers into logical groups from which you can isolate new sales opportunities and develop account plans to move on them. For you, the outcome is increased income per customer. For your customers, the outcome is more effective and personalized coverage from someone local they can trust.

My seminars and workshops have helped thousands of agencies of all sizes implement the RFA System successfully. What they discovered is that if they follow through and stay true to the process, it's a success. I've watched agents rediscover their love of this business. They're no longer sitting in their offices just filling out paperwork; they're out there talking to customers again. And when they are doing paperwork, their customers are sitting next to them while they do it.

Veteran agents aren't the only ones I've watched become energized. New agents with small books of business have also implemented the RFA System with great success. In fact, I've watched newer agents who took advantage of the RFA System grow their businesses far more quickly than they otherwise could have—even though they have fewer customers than the average agency. I've read the letters and e-mails, and taken calls from agents using the RFA System. There is no doubt: The system works. And yes, the system applies to both existing customers as well as new customers. I'll touch on how to handle potential customers later, but for right now let's focus on how to handle your existing customer base.

# SEGMENT YOUR CUSTOMERS
## TO FIND THE GOLD

The first step in the RFA System requires you to segment your customers. You'll be sorting your clients into three segments, beginning with "Group A" customers. Those are the customers you or someone on your staff knows by name. Sit down with your staff to compile your list, then sort them by the kind of policies they have with your agency. List as many Group A customers as possible, which should be relatively easy to do because you shouldn't have to look anywhere. You're only after the people who spring right to mind. Typically, they're the customers with whom you have the strongest relationships.

The next segment, "Group B" customers, includes those who have placed more than one product line with your agency. You'll probably have a lot of customers on this list who are also in the Group A category. However, only customers who aren't already in Group A should be listed in Group B.

From the third category, the "Group C" customers, list all those in your book of business who have only a single product line with your agency. The easiest way to do this is to sort your database and print out product line customers. Group C customers are those who are most "at risk." They probably have other relationships in the insurance and financial services area and are most likely to leave. They also contribute the least to your bottom line because of the disproportionate attention and resources you must expend to administer this single product line. In other words, people who fall into Group C are your least profitable customers.

Now, look at the customers in Group A (those well known to the agency). Rank them by product lines per household, putting those with the most product lines at the top, and moving down your list to those with the fewest product lines at the bottom. For an example, see "Gap Analysis, Part 1" in **Appendix Three**.

Next, look at the customers in Group B (those with more than one product line) and rank them by the most product lines per household.

After you've completed this exercise you should know the nature of your customer reach and how strong your relationships are. The fun part comes next, because you now have the tools to take back your agency. You're in control again. You have your customers prioritized. You have a list of which customers to meet with first. You have the basis for a marketing plan built around the customers who most trust and respect you—Group A and Group B customers.

## Capitalize on Targets of Opportunity

Before you leap into action, refine your list one more time. Look at all the households you identified with more than one product. Identify which products are missing in those households; they represent your most likely prospects. For an example, see "Gap Analysis, Part 2—What's Missing?" in **Appendix Three**.

Once your customers have been segmented as described above, sales opportunities become evident. Now it's easy to launch a targeted campaign using customized marketing letters. Auto and fire should be a "no brainer" in terms of marketing focus. You pick the products you want to market and match the customers who don't have those products with you. The key is that now you know specifically who to market to. Start with auto and fire. (See **Appendix Three** for sample marketing letters.)

The next logical target consists of all those clients who don't have life insurance placed with your agency. These customers probably have some life insurance, whether through their work or placed with another company. However, my research indicates that most people are inadequately covered when it comes to life insurance. What an open field! In fact, it's safe to say that in most agencies the prospects for life insurance include just about every client. Even agents who think they're doing a superior job of selling life insurance typically only penetrate 10-15 percent of their multiple-line book of business. So even there, you'll find lots of room for improvement in this area—and huge opportunities!

Your next exciting focus would be umbrellas. A great way to block the mono-line auto companies from stealing your customers is to surround them with other products. Umbrella coverage is becoming more common as jury awards get higher and people have more assets to protect. This is good for the client, good for retention, and also good for your agency because umbrella coverage typically requires that customers have their auto insurance with you as well.

What next? Investment products. I'm convinced the future for multiple-line agents requires that a full range of products be offered not only for asset protection, but for asset accumulation as well. See Chapter 12 for much more about how to increase customer retention and solidify your customer relationships by offering investment products.

Meanwhile, don't overlook the importance of complementary products such as auto loans, home loans, auto mechanical breakdown or home warranty coverage. All of them offer tremendous value to your customers. Your carrier may or may not offer these products at the time you're reading this book. If they're not, you can be assured that in order to stay competitive they will be adding these companion products in the near future.

Finally, you might want to include in your marketing efforts what I call a "fun to insure" letter. Today's families live active lifestyles. Most own multiple TV sets, a computer or two, and lots of sophisticated "toys" such as snowmobiles, boats, houseboats, run-abouts, ATVs, motor homes, campers, and the like. Why shouldn't you be their insurer of choice for the fun stuff? Indeed, sending a letter that asks such a question also conveys the message that you're a multipurpose agent with versatile products. In turn, your customers will increasingly see your agency as the only one they need for all their insurance and financial services needs. Talk about your home runs!

## Develop an Account Plan

Before you call to set appointments with your Group A and Group B customers, I strongly suggest that you develop an account plan for each one. I developed an account plan method modeled after successful commercial brokers who use this strategy with their large customers. The underlying philosophy is that every household account, regardless of size, deserves personal attention and excellent service. It's how you add value and differentiate yourself from the competition. Specific points to consider for your household account plan:

1. Determine how many customer contacts you will make in a year. The contacts can come from letters, phone calls, or personal visits.

2. Add customers to birthday card lists, holiday card lists, etc.

3. Add customers to your newsletter mailing list.

4. Expand your efforts with specialty marketing campaigns. Ideas include sending an ice cream certificate in the summer, a gift certificate for lunch at a local restaurant, a holiday gift basket, and the like.

5. Target customers for special occasions. It's a strategy particularly well-suited for commercial accounts. For example, provide pizza for an office gathering so you can make a lasting impression and seize the opportunity to begin the relationship-building process with the account holder's employees.

You'll find an Account Plan Checklist in **Appendix Three**. You can use it as is, or adapt it to meet your own specific needs.

Once you've set an account plan for each household, put your plan into action. Schedule appointments to meet with each customer to review his or her needs and deepen the relationship. When you do that, notice how much fun the interaction is. You're talking to customers who value your advice and appreciate your interest. They're the ones you enjoy being with. They are the gold from within your database.

You may have some households with five or six products placed with your agency. Terrific! How would you characterize the relationship you have with the members of these households? Probably excellent, right? The goal is to build more households just like them.

The Account Plan Checklist will help keep you focused on the goals you set for each household. Work this system every day for 90 days, then review your results. You'll be surprised at the progress you'll make in achieving your focus goals—while having fun in the process.

The beauty of the RFA System is that it puts you in control of your agency. You decide which households to tackle first. You decide on the components of a plan to deepen the relationship with your customer. Honestly? If you've been frustrated over the lack of growth in your agency, the results you'll achieve with the RFA System may well be the turning point to make it take off.

# Group C Customers

So what about those Group C customers? How do you approach a single product-line customer where the relationship is minor, to say the least, and build on that fragile foundation? Well, first you have to determine if the mono-line customer wants more of the products you offer or just plain doesn't care.

It's easy to let cynicism get in your way and assume the worst, but don't let that happen. Remember, in retooling your agency you committed to retooling your own mindset as well. Let that work for you! No matter what your previous relationship with Group C customers, start with the optimistic assumption that at least some of those people can be converted to long-term clients interested in building a relationship with you. After all, it could be that some of your Group C customers haven't been showing interest because their lives are so frenetic that they've grown overwhelmed to the point of paralysis in their personal financial dealings. It could also be that they've become jaded in general with all kinds of business associations. I talked about that early in the book, and mono-line customers might have experienced the pinch of skepticism more than others.

No matter what the case, you need to make a good-faith effort to bring wayward customers into the fold. Start by having your agency contact representative (ACR) call each Group C customer to set an appointment with you. The annual review is an ideal tool because for hesitant customers it might sound more like "business as usual" than a straightforward sales call. What you're after is some face time to start cultivating a relationship, so a non-threatening approach is your best bet.

Some will surprise you by agreeing to an appointment. But don't relax yet. Of all your customers, those in the Group C category are most likely to be no-shows. When that happens—and it will—don't bail on them yet. Get back in touch and find out why they didn't come in. See if you can reschedule. Some of them may have had a legitimate conflict and simply forgot to call. But with others, what you might learn is that at some point they experienced a problem with your agency but never actually expressed it. Indeed, they may have only perceived a problem. Either way, take immediate steps to resolve whatever issue might be lurking behind their reluctance to meet with you. If that doesn't work and their resistance remains strong, don't knock yourself out trying to win them over. It won't happen. If they had no complaints but tell you their only interest is in rock-bottom prices, don't try to persuade them otherwise. They won't listen.

Bottom line? For the truly reluctant mono-line customers, continue to service their accounts with the same professionalism you show to all your customers. Your focus for these customers should be to give them the service they desire and have every right to expect. However, they've already shown you they don't care to expand their relationship with you, so no additional marketing action is needed for these households. You will now have more time to focus on your A, B, and—yes, your C—customers who want to deepen their relationship with your office.

Those mono-line customers who make an appointment and do

follow up obviously suggest at least some interest in listening to what you have to say. Make them glad they came in. Don't push product at them, but update their information and find out what their needs are. Let them know what options are available. Mostly, let them get to know you better—to begin to see you as a trusted partner for their insurance and financial needs. Make sure you get to know them better, too. Look, they may never be the "stars" in your database, but that doesn't mean they won't surprise you with opportunities. You'd be foolish not to give them the old college try.

## Take the Next Step Out

With all your customers, what you're looking for is a "touch point," an opportunity to meet with them and take the next step in your agency plan. The touch point may be an annual review, it could be the need to review life coverage, or whatever. While you're meeting to review a specific customer need, it's important that you identify beforehand what other gaps may exist in this household. Once you address the specific product the customer came to discuss, you'll want to raise the issue of which products he or she doesn't have placed with your agency. The discussion must be launched from the perspective of the person's current needs, then segueing into other possible needs and the ways you can help. You're using the product sale to improve the relationship.

That's just the opposite of the way everybody else looks at it.

## ONE MORE TIME, WITH FEELING— THE CUSTOMER CONCIERGE

We all know it's easy to get distracted from accomplishing important tasks. It's hard to keep things from sliding when the phone is ringing and there are customers "on hold" or waiting in the lobby to keep their appointments with you. But I hope you'll adopt my premise that no file is put away until the database is updated and the file is calendared for the next step. Remember, your calendar is the ultimate pending system. You can't let daily interruptions thwart you and your staff from using it to schedule follow-ups.

### A TYPICAL CLIENT SITUATION

*A customer, Mrs. Fernandez, calls the office to change her auto insurance to cover a new car purchase. In the course of the conversation, she mentions that she will keep her old car in the garage for three months until her 17-year-old son gets his driver's license.*

*Someone must enter this important information into the database and calendar it for follow-up in 70 days, when Mrs. Fernandez will need an auto policy for her son. Mrs. Fernandez will appreciate your attention to detail and feel like a valued customer because you kept track of a milestone event in her family's life.*

The whole notion of shoving aside interruptions to keep your database current sounds like a tall order, doesn't it? But there is a way out of the distraction challenge, and it's by making a specific individual in your office accountable to complete database updating and household calendaring on a daily basis. That's right; I said accountable. Let's face it, nothing seems to happen unless somebody is responsible for making sure that what's important gets done. Thus, although I've said it before, I'm saying it again: Create a staff position for a customer concierge, and fill it with a responsible person you're confident you can regard as your primary customer advocate. Having a concierge doesn't give the rest of your staff license to ignore customer service, of course, but employing a concierge guarantees that nothing falls through the cracks. That's because the primary focus of the concierge is to facilitate the account plan for each household. You'll recall that in addition to following up with database updating and calendaring, it's the concierge who subsequently contacts customers to make sure the service they received met or exceeded their expectations.

What happens next? Assuming your customer did indeed receive satisfactory or better service, you want a moment of that customer's time in order to update your database information so you can serve him even better. Use the Household Update Sheet, which includes all the products you sell and all the ways to contact customers. Most customers are more than happy to provide the information because they're pleased with the "special" service and attention they just received. The personalized contact virtually guarantees improved retention and helps you identify and weed out any potential problems.

In the end, it's the customer concierge who should be your gate-keeper of information. Spend time with your staff and account executives to stress the importance of constantly and consistently gathering client information to forward to the concierge. I recommend using electronic files and setting up a system for subsequent customer contacts. You may be able to program your computer along with your insurance company to create a system that will automatically do queries and assist you in sending out systematic letters. Check into that possibility before creating your own system. Just make sure that whether you're using a company's proprietary database or "off-the-shelf" software, you immediately invest time in making sure your entries are done consistently and that you're not double entering the data.

## How Often Should You "Touch" Customers?

In today's market, you simply cannot contact your customer too often. Customers will never leave you because you gave them too much attention. It's only when they feel neglected that they seek solutions elsewhere. When that happens your value proposition decreases and price becomes the only differential—a losing strategy.

I urge that you "touch" your customer at least seven times a year. For example, send a letter every other month to households that you've targeted for specific products. In addition you'll want to make a minimum of one outbound phone call—preferably two—to each household. Outbound calls don't include calls that your customer makes to you.

When preparing to make an outbound call, think about the specific customer. Even if you've spoken with this customer and updated his or her household information, it's still important to stay in touch. Staying in touch could be as simple as dropping a line such as, "Hope all is well." Or you could phone and leave a message, saying, "Just checking in to make sure all is well with you and your family. If you have any questions or need assistance on any of your insurance or financial services products, give me a call." Mind you, it's not just important to stay in touch with every single customer. It's critical. If you think I'm overstating my case, just try to remember the last time any of your own service providers—a doctor, a dentist, or a stockbroker, for instance—contacted you to inquire how you were doing. You're probably hard put to come up with anyone. Imagine, though, how fast you'd gravitate to those who did? Staying in touch sends a powerful message about caring, and people gravitate toward people who care about them.

There's another benefit, of course. The more you and your agency are "top of the mind," the more you can block out the competition. Seal enduring relationships with your customers by letting the concierge be their advocate, then touch them with regularity, and you'll develop clients committed to you—and eager to grow with your agency.

# Use the RFA System for New Customers, Too

The Relationship-Focused Agency System is really all about connecting with people, listening to them, and capturing the information they provide. I've already shown you how to use it for existing customers, but the RFA System is every bit as robust for new customers. You simply begin by sitting down with new clients and taking them through a series of questions to try and learn as much as you can about their lifestyles, their families, and their financial goals. It's an information-gathering exercise, really.

For that matter, the whole business of gathering information brings up a critical issue, especially for the property and casualty agent. Where did we ever come up with the notion not to ask too many detailed questions of our customers, especially as it relates to their assets? We're not saying that everybody in the industry shies away from asking pertinent questions. On the other hand, I've definitely witnessed a level of unease in getting specific information on all customer assets in the process of writing a homeowners, automobile insurance, or other P&C policy. The problem with being timid is this: How can you properly determine the appropriate level of coverage on an automobile insurance policy without knowing the size of the customer's total assets? Some of you might be saying, "Isn't that what umbrella insurance is for?" Sure it is, but our customers need to be protected so that their savings don't have to be tapped as a result of poor initial coverage.

## PROBE DEEPLY

Too often when we take our customers' information over the phone, we fail to probe deeply enough, and we neglect to make sure they understand why we're asking for specifics in the first place. In fact, most property and casualty agents have conditioned their customers to give them the least amount of information. The customers respond in kind, because they fear that the more information they give an insurance agent the higher their rates will climb. But ultimately, our business is not about rates; it's about making sure that we protect the assets of our customers in case of loss. So ask the questions that need to be asked. Get the details on their financial situation. Ask them about their home, their cars, their lifestyle, their "toys," their bank account, stocks and other securities—all the assets they hold. Don't overlook inquiring whether they own a vacation home or rental property. Get them to disclose as much as you can.

No doubt you've heard it said that before you can build your assets you must protect what you already have. Make sure you do this for your customer. However, don't get sucked into complicated systems or "touchy-feely" programs that don't move you and your clients toward sales. Just focus on what I'm suggesting—gathering information and leveraging it into a sales opportunity.

## A Final Word

If you use the RFA System, you'll soon wonder how you ever coped without it. But the RFA System isn't something you do once and then put away. It's a process, and for any process to work for maximum effectiveness it has to be used. So stay in front of your customers with "face time." Letters? Post cards? Birthday cards? They're great and you should use them to your advantage. However, never forget that your customers still need to hear from you. They need to know you care, and to see you as one of their personal consultants—those local, trusted people with whom they feel comfortable discussing private information.

Your customers are no different than you are. You feel comfortable with people you're in contact with. You probably don't feel very comfortable with those who don't bother to call you. It's just human nature.

The RFA System works. I know, because I put it in place in my own agency and got outstanding results. I've included all the tools you need to successfully implement RFA into your agency, too. Your job? Get out there and use them!

# Chapter Highlights

— The Relationship-Focused Agency System will help you redefine the value proposition you offer to your customers and, more importantly, boost your agency from one focused on product sales to one focused on building relationships—a key to deeper household penetration.

— The RFA System leads your staff to the next step while gathering the information to continually update the database. In turn, you get a never-ending source of sales leads and possibilities.

— There is gold in them thar hills—if you know where to dig. Start by segmenting your customers into groups based on the depth of the relationships you have with them.

— Complete a "gap analysis" to determine the quality of the relationships you have with your customers.

— Capitalize instantly on targets of opportunity, and use "touch points" to help fill the gaps.

— Develop an account plan for each household; it's all part of the system and working the RFA System puts you in control.

— Work with mono-line customers who indicate a willingness

to listen to what you have to say. Don't spend an undue amount of time on those who balk.

— Appoint a customer concierge to make sure your customers never have to settle for anything less than the best. A concierge anticipates customer needs and takes accountability for making sure your database is up to date.

— Dealing with new customers is a golden opportunity to use the RFA System to build a solid relationship from the get-go. Don't shy away from targeted questions. Details are critical if you're to provide your customers with the coverage they genuinely need.

— To maximize the benefits of the RFA System, use it every day!

# RETOOLING YOUR STAFF TRAINING AND RECRUITING

CHAPTER | TEN

Over the last several chapters, I've tried to demonstrate how you can retool your agency for greater success. Unfortunately, you won't be able to put any of my methods into play if you don't build a great staff. That's true even if you have only one employee. If you have great staff members, they need to transition to the specialist model and become true advocates of your agency. But in order to change, they must focus on customer service and have excellent follow-up techniques. Remember, you want each member of your staff to be a profit center, not a cost center. To make sure that happens, you have to train your staff to leverage every customer contact.

In this chapter I'll provide you with a strategy to retool your staff. Start by evaluating your existing staff. Look for these five key qualities in each person:

1. Wants to grow professionally and personally;

2. Has a positive attitude;

3. Is a hard worker;

4. Has a sense of urgency;

5. Shows pride in his or her work.

See a sample Employee Evaluation Form in **Appendix Three** that you can tailor to your agency's specific needs. The form also provides documentation for your employee file.

# Retool Your Existing Staff Training

As you recall, the specialist model requires each of your staff members to focus on one area and become an expert in it. Futhermore, each of them must be able to deliver great service and turn service calls into sales by gathering additional information from customers, identifying customer needs, and suggesting appropriate solutions. But your staff members will have different strengths and weaknesses, so training everyone the same way is counterproductive. You must focus on the individual.

Start by doing an assessment of each member of your staff. The assessment should focus first on whether each employee is proactive or reactive. Many agents believe they have great staff members because they're good at handling service calls. But there's a difference between a staff member who is proactive and one who is reactive. The reactive staff person does her job well, but once the specific request has been handled, she stops there, thinking it's acceptable to do only what is expected.

The proactive staff person takes the situation to the next level. You know if you have a proactive staff person if you get a lot of positive feedback about how that person wowed the customer by going above and beyond what was expected.

## THE HUMAN TOUCH

*I love to observe my office director, Sharon Jansma, when she is working with clients. She can take someone who is upset and put them totally at ease. There is an art to advanced customer service. The client doesn't even know what is happening. All they know is that Sharon makes them feel like the most important person in the world. She restates their issues and meets them right where they are coming from. She then takes them by the hand and shows them the way forward to a mutually satisfactory solution. The customer knows that without a doubt someone cares. I often have people call me after their experience to share with me their complete satisfaction with doing business with my office.*

*Your odds of complete customer satisfaction are at peak levels when you take this approach.*

Unfortunately, proactive staff people are hard to find. However, that doesn't mean you have to fire your existing people. You just have to train them to be proactive. Here's what you need to teach them to focus on:

— Taking customer service to the "AWESOME!!" level;

—   Improving communication techniques, such as learning to listen, learning to ask follow-up questions, and learning to build relationships;

—   Turning information into follow-up sales opportunities.

Here's an example on how to do the latter. Assume that Mr. Smith has just called in to make a change in his auto policy. During the conversation with a customer service representative, he mentions that his family is building a cabin in the mountains because they enjoy skiing. To shift Mr. Smith's routine call into a follow-up sales opportunity, the conversation would go something like this:

**CSR:** That must be exciting! When will construction be completed?
**Mr. Smith:** About 60 days.
**CSR:** That's great! I see that we already carry your homeowners insurance. When is a good time to set up a homeowners policy on your new cabin?
**Mr. Smith:** I've been meaning to talk with you about that. I need proof of insurance for my mortgage company. I can come in next Tuesday.
**CSR:** Is morning or afternoon better for you?
**Mr. Smith:** Ten in the morning works for me.
**CSR:** We'll see you next Tuesday at 10 a.m. And in the meantime, I'll take care of your auto change. Thanks for your business, Mr. Smith, and congratulations on your new cabin.

Your employees won't learn these techniques in a day or a week. Training must be ongoing. It also must be done in a cooperative fashion. Adults learn best by doing and personalizing the experience. Here's what I suggest: When you first commit to change your agency from a generalist to a specialist model, set aside an hour a day for two weeks and devote that time exclusively to staff training. As the staff gains more proficiency, you can cut back your training schedule to one day per week.

Start with proactive customer service. To do that effectively, you must empower your staff. Rename the CSR position to "customer advocate (CA)." The title of customer advocate is a powerful and personal term that subtly but instantly tells your customers they have someone always looking out for them. It also tells your staff that your priority is resolving people problems, not just servicing accounts. Get your CA to treat customers as family. One way to do that is to ask each employee to obtain photos of the customers they deal with, or have a digital camera on hand for photo opportunities when a customer stops by. Run a contest that rewards the employee who collects the most photos. Encourage each specialist to display these photos in his or her work space to further personalize every customer interaction. Your objective is to train your employees to view each customer as an individual.

Model your agency after the best customer service companies

such as Nordstrom, The Four Seasons Hotels, or a local business known for superior customer service. Have your staff members practice the techniques they're learning. You'll find some specific topics and strategies for effective staff training further down in this chapter. Meanwhile, understand that not every person enjoys dealing with people. For that reason, only employees who are "people persons" should be talking with your customers. You probably already know who they are.

Next, to help your staff members improve their ability to build relationships with customers, move on to training that will improve their communication techniques such as learning to listen and asking follow-up questions. To start, first describe what you want the outcome to be—a sales opportunity—then work back from that point. In order to become a good communicator, you must first make sure your employees understand what poor communication is, then build from there. Following is an example of poor communications:

*"Good morning, John Jones Insurance."*

*"Hello, this is Carol Smith. I just purchased a new car and need to change my auto insurance."*

*"John's not in. Can I have him call you?"*

*"Yes, please. My number is 555-9393.*

*"Okay, thanks."*

Amazingly enough, limp conversations like this occur all too often. Look at all the missed opportunities. The employee wasn't very cordial, didn't seek any information, and didn't deepen the customer relationship. All the employee did was take a phone message.

Now let's look at the same situation using good communication skills.

> "Good morning, John Jones Insurance and Financial Services. How may I direct your call?"
>
> "Hello, this is Carol Smith. I just purchased a new car and need to change my auto insurance."
>
> "Congratulations on your new purchase, Mrs. Smith! Let me connect you with Abbey Johnson. She's one of our customer advocates and can take care of your needs. One moment, please."
>
> "Hello, Mrs. Smith, this is Abbey Johnson. I hear you just bought a new car. That's terrific! What did you buy?"
>
> "I bought a new Lexus."
>
> "That's great! I remember that you once mentioned you really liked the Lexus. What color did you get?" (Shows interest in the customer, thus deepening the relationship.)
>
> "Silver gray, just like I wanted."
>
> "I'm so happy for you. I'm glad that you got exactly what

*you wanted." (Abbey takes down the pertinent information*
*to make the switch in coverage and asks if coverage for the*
*customer's previous auto is still necessary.)*

*"Mrs. Smith, while I've got you on the phone, were you*
*aware that we now offer financial services, such as mutual*
*funds, annuities, and savings plans for retirement?"*

*"Really! I've been thinking about setting up college funds for*
*my three grandchildren. Do you handle accounts like that?"*

*"Yes, of course. Mr. Jones can sit down with you and go over*
*several options for your consideration. What would be a*
*good time to get together here at the office, Tuesday or*
*Thursday?"*

*"Tuesday is best for me."*

*"Let me check Mr. Jones' calendar. Tuesday works for him,*
*too. Can you make it at 10 a.m. or 2:30 p.m.?*

*"Tuesday at 10 o'clock is fine."*

*"Great! We'll see you here at 10 a.m. on Tuesday, the 19th.*
*Be sure to drive your new car. I can't wait to see it. And*
*thank you, Mrs. Smith. We appreciate your business."*

Notice how the customer advocate turned information into a
follow-up opportunity? From your perspective, mining a conversation for openers is probably the easiest thing for your staff to
grasp. After all, it's what you do as an insurance professional. You

listen and identify your customers' needs and then you offer the appropriate solutions. The sale follows from there. However, just because it's easy for you, don't assume it's easy to teach or that your customer advocates will have an immediate comfort level in distilling new information from a call that begins with a mundane conversation. It takes practice, and that's where role playing comes in.

## BUILD CONFIDENCE WITH ROLE PLAYING

The beauty of role playing is that it's non-threatening. Your customer advocates can build confidence within the comfort zone of your own office staff. If they forget something or muff a line, you're right there to help them smooth over the rough spots. It's a matter of practice and when you schedule role-playing sessions, try a variety of scenarios typical of what your customer advocates might experience on the phone with a real customer. You or another staff member can play the role of the customer. You may want to provide a script with key points or phrases to be used in every conversation with a customer.

To optimize role-playing sessions, tape them so your customer advocates can hear the phrases that work effectively, and those that may need to be refined. The process builds self-assurance, so when the CA speaks with a customer, the words and appropriate phrases flow automatically. Practice until they master the techniques using a step-by-step approach. At the very least you must get every staff member to learn to refer a call to someone else in the agency if he or she can't perform a given task or isn't trained on a particular product line.

## RECOGNIZING "TRIGGERS"

When Benjamin Franklin quipped, "In this world, nothing is certain but death and taxes," he was right on the money. But if he'd been an insurance agent, he might have further speculated on events that are *almost* certain—and certainly valid enough for you to consider when you're trying to flush out information from your customers. I'm talking about the kinds of major changes that occur in almost everyone's life, and broadly speaking those changes fall into three categories: work, family, and money. Following is an example of five pivotal changes in each category.

| Work | Family | Money |
|---|---|---|
| Change in job or career | Marriage or divorce | Buy or sell a house |
| Promotion | Start a family | Purchase a vacation home |
| Relocation | College for a child | Investment gain or loss |
| Start or end a business | Injury or illness | Serious debt |
| Retirement | Caring for a parent | Inheritance or windfall |

Obviously, some transitions are happy events. Others are traumatic. Some are short-term events, while others are long-term. Prompt your staff to probe gently during the course of conversations with customers, and in the process to try and learn whether your customers even anticipate a life-altering change. For instance, if a customer mentions that one day he'd love to move to another area of town, make sure your CA doesn't assume the customer is just "thinking out loud" or expressing a pipe dream. Encourage your CA to learn whether the customer foresees such a move in the next year—or even three years down the road. Residual changes could spiral off the first. For example, your customer's motivation in moving might be based on his concern that in the future he'll need to be closer to his aging parents, who already live in the area he mentioned. A move and the need to take on a care-giving role may well mean that your customer will require more coverage than he already has. Those changes may occur in the future, but anticipating them now means you'll be ready when your customer is, and you'll be able to steer him toward the insurance he needs.

Remind your staff that they're aiming for customer-focused relationship building, which calls for everyone to take a genuine and consistent interest in customers and their families. Ours is a people business, and the more you and your staff show interest in your customers, the more loyal those customers will be. The potential for you is another sale. The potential for your customer is additional security.

## REWARD ACHIEVERS

Now that you've got some tools to help you train your staff in identifying sales opportunities, how can you keep them fired up? Easy! Challenge them to play the game, "Who can gather the most information?" Every time a CA gleans information from a customer that could lead to a sales opportunity, ask the CA to write the customer name and his or her own name on a slip of paper. At the end of the day, deposit these slips into a box. Once a week, count up the CA slips in the box and present a prize to the CA who has gathered the most information. The prize could be a pair of theater tickets, lunch or dinner for two, or a pre-selected cash prize. A contest is merely a way to keep at the top of your mind your agency's goal to gather information and seek out sales opportunities. You'll be amazed at the results.

# Training Topics

All of your staff training efforts are directed toward expanding relationships with your customers, and in the process, identifying opportunities for new sales. As you've seen, some of the training you'll undertake with your staff involves conceptual issues, such as understanding what constitutes a trigger during the course of

conversations with customers. Those conceptual issues are funda-
mental to driving your agency forward, but don't overlook smaller
or more routine training topics in the process. Here are some
subject areas that I've found essential in making sure business
is conducted in a professional, helpful, and uniform manner:

### 1) Phone Etiquette

How do your employees answer the phone? Write an
appropriate script and train every employee to answer the
phone using the same words every day, every time.
Consistency is key.

### 2) Customer Service

You need to articulate your expectations for customer service.
Set procedures and standards for quoting, how quickly
customer follow-up is made, and so on. Customer satisfaction
must be the focus. Teach your staff to incorporate the following into every customer service conversation:

— using the customer's name;
— restating the question to ensure comprehension;
— being sure to say "thank you."

### 3) Learning People Skills/Techniques

Courtesy and respect are the name of the game. Everyone
likes to hear his or her name spoken, so instruct your staff to

call your customers by name. But be careful. Set guidelines on when and if it's appropriate to use a customer's first name. You don't want your staff members to be perceived as overly familiar. The Golden Rule certainly applies here. Treat others as you would have them treat you.

## 4) Creative Problem-Solving

Every day brings new challenges. As a result of this simple truth, you and your key staff members must be creative problem solvers. One approach is to set aside problems until a specific time every day, call a quick staff meeting, and brainstorm solutions for each situation. Delegate a staff person to follow up on each problem until it is solved.

## 5) Identify the "Next Action"

Teach your staff to lead every customer conversation to the "next action" to penetrate more deeply into that household. The next action may be as simple as calendaring a phone call in three months to set a meeting about life insurance. Or it could be calendaring a date when you know a teenager in the family will be getting a driver's license. No matter what the event, the path to agency growth is to focus on the next action you will take with each client.

### 6) Use "COPS" to Seek Information On Every Customer Contact

Train your staff to use my Customer Opportunity Profile System (COPS) to keep every customer file current. COPS is a system that I've developed into a handy form, which provides key phrases for your staff to use such as, "I want to make sure we have the proper information in your file." The COPS form also includes space for product notes, trigger events, and more. It's a simple system, but it works like a charm. You'll find the COPS form in **Appendix Three**. Feel free to print it and make multiple copies for each staff member.

## Retool Your Staff Recruiting

You will lose staff. If you've been in business for any amount of time, you know how true this is. Losing staff is probably the single most devastating situation to happen in your agency. You can survive rate hikes, moratoriums, and service problems with your writing company or companies. But losing a staff member, especially a key one, can bring your agency to a halt and make your life miserable. Unfortunately, many agents wait until after the staff person has given notice before they begin looking for a replacement. By then it's too late.

## PROACTIVE RECRUITING

You must have a plan for when you lose a staff person. Your approach should include a contingency plan for short-term reassignment of duties among yourself and the remaining staff. You should also have a list of candidates you've already identified as potential hires—people who would join your agency given the opportunity. What that means is that you must constantly be recruiting, letting people know there's always a place for talented people at your agency. Ask your customers for referrals; they'll be honored you value your relationship with them enough to seek their input. Let people in your local community know you're always looking for outstanding people. Pay bonuses to your staff members if they refer people. In other words, set up a referral system for new employees. If you go the distance with advance recruiting, there's no reason you'll ever have to settle for second best.

## GETTING THE RIGHT KIND OF TALENT

You want people who will be as committed to you as you are to them, so make sure from the outset that everyone you talk to about an employment opportunity understands that working at your agency is a privilege. You're not just talking to candidates about a job. You're talking about a career with growth potential and the opportunity to advance and increase their income.

When do you start the interview process? Before you even need to make a hire! Even if you don't currently have a position available, interview everyone referred to you. Tell them up front that you currently don't have any positions available, but that you have a growing agency and there will be positions in the future.

During your conversations, listen to what applicants say they are looking for in a job. You don't want someone just interested in a paycheck. You need to see passion, excitement. My favorite question is, "If you had a magic wand and could create any job, what would it be? Describe in detail what it is about your dream job that is so appealing to you." If the answer is all about needing a job to make money, that's not an applicant for you. An applicant who describes specific tasks or end results that focus on dealing with people and customer service is one who should pique your interest.

Once you're interested in a person, invite him or her to your agency to talk to everyone in the office. Your staff will know what questions to ask and the input they offer will be very insightful. After this process is complete, discuss with your staff members whether they would hire the applicant. If everyone is in agreement, contact the applicant and congratulate him or her on being accepted for placement on your potential agency team list. Follow up with a nice note and put the person on your list for mailings about your agency, as well as for a birthday card. In other words, stay in touch.

Rank the people on your list. On the day that a valued staff person announces that he or she must leave your agency (and it will happen), you can grab your list and start calling people you already know want to work with you, and they'll be the people you and your staff have already agreed would be great additions.

## Quick-Start: Training New Staff Members

Once you've hired a new staff person, you need to start the training process right away. In fact, don't let the new hire interact with customers until you're confident he'll be able to provide great customer service.

At most, the initial training process should run ten days. Have the new employee start on a Friday. On that day he should sit with each staff member and learn exactly what everybody does. Ask your new hire to come in on Saturday and use that day (a slow one) to become familiar with the systems, procedures, and other administrative aspects of the office that are difficult to learn when the phones are ringing off the hook. Saturday training should be conducted by you or your office director, if you have one.

On Monday, have your new employee spend the day with the staff member he'll be replacing. You'll almost always have a comfortable period of time in which to get your new person started before your current employee leaves. However, if timing is such that your existing staff member has already left when the new person starts, designate as the trainer a trusted staff member who's familiar with the position functions. Of course, you don't want your substitute staffer to fall behind in her own responsibilities, so call up your contingency plan for short-term reassignment of duties. It may not be as elegant or convenient for getting a new person started, but it'll safely carry you through the interim with minimal interruption in the normal flow of business.

Tuesday is boss training day and your new recruit spends the whole day with you. He'll see what you do and how you handle clients. This is your chance to teach your new employee what the values of your agency are. The process gives your new hire an opportunity to see the "big picture" and all the different facets that go into running an agency. It helps him connect the dots about how he fits into the overall scheme of things.

## SPENDING A DAY WITH THE BOSS

*I enjoy introducing a new employee to our customers. It makes the employee feel valued and demonstrates to the customer that our agency is thriving. The introduction goes something like this: "This is Jan Jones. She'll be handling homeowners customer service once she completes her training. Would you mind if Jan sits in our meeting today? I want her to get a broad view of all the facets of our agency operation." (The employee observes, but does not participate in the meeting).*

*After the client leaves, I answer any questions Jan has, then we repeat the process with the next customer appointment. By the end of the day, Jan has observed presentations for a wide variety of products and should have copious notes on key phrases used in client presentations. She has also witnessed the uncommon courtesy and respect we show our customers. She's then ready for the next step, role playing.*

Frequently evaluate the new hire's work performance for the first 30 days. If he isn't performing up to the expectations you set, terminate him. Don't hope things will get better. They won't. Go back to your list and find the next person. A poorly performing employee can do more damage to your agency than having no employee at all.

If the employee is meeting the expectations you've set, continue to evaluate his performance at regular intervals, at least twice a year. The employee will become more and more valuable as he gains day-to-day experience and gets to know your customers.

# Chapter Highlights

— Your staff is critical to moving your agency forward. Evaluate every employee. Does each one meet the five-way test?

— In today's competitive market, it's not enough for an employee to have a pleasant telephone voice and a courteous disposition. Your staff members need to be proactive. Teach them to seek more information and go beyond what is expected. Reward achievers!

— Training needs to be a continual process. Involve your staff in role playing. It's a non-threatening way to speed the process and build confidence. Don't overlook training topics that can take your staff to the next level.

— Teach your staff to identify trigger events in the lives of your customers. Consistently showing interest in your customers promotes loyalty—and that leads to increased sales!

— Recruit new staff *before* you have an actual vacancy. Make a point of routinely getting referrals from a variety of sources, and develop a list of qualified candidates. Talk to them before you need to fill a position.

— Quick-start new staff training in a ten-day process—including a day in which your new hire spends the day with you to get the big picture.

PROFIT FROM CHANGE

# PART FOUR

# ENSURING YOUR FUTURE

PROFIT FROM CHANGE

# JUMP-START YOUR NEW CUSTOMER GROWTH

# CHAPTER ELEVEN

In the last several chapters I've described a system that allows you to better leverage your staff and existing customer relationships and take your agency to new levels of productivity and profits. Now I'll show you how to grow your agency fast with the right new customers.

The first thing you have to know? Conventional X-dating is dead! In fact, anyone who tells you that cold call X-dating works hasn't been on the phone in years. That doesn't mean that an X-date isn't still a powerful piece of information. However, the customary method of getting that information is outdated.

Customers today are extremely savvy when it comes to avoiding sales calls. For one thing, millions have signed up for the Federal Trade Commission's "Do Not Call Registry," which prohibits blatantly uninvited sales calls to their homes and cell phones. The FTC is tough on penalizing violators, so you need to make sure you aren't one of them. Verify that you're in compliance not only with federal rules on who you can or can't call, but any state or local rules that may apply as well. Periodically review and prune your lists as needed. Of course, even consumers who haven't put their names on the Do Not Call Registry can spot sales calls from a mile away. They're harder to reach than ever, and even if you do reach them they typically just hang up.

Let's face it, the traditional method of X-dating requires you to be a beggar. You have to call people you don't know and beg them for information about when their auto and home policies will expire. Hit rates are very low. The work is tedious at best, and demoralizing in most instances. Potential customers are simply viewed as single product buyers. Get in, make your pitch, get out with a sale. The result? You limit your information gathering because you don't want to jeopardize the specific sale with the X-date call. It's why traditional X-dating has never been a sustainable growth engine.

Understandably, a lot of agents decrease or discontinue cold calling on X-dates once their agency begins to generate enough revenue to survive. New business then only comes in through referrals. If you're like most agents, you like referral business. You're no longer a beggar; a potential customer is calling you. He or she might not know you personally, but someone has said you're a good agent. You're beginning your relationship from a positive position of strength.

Unfortunately, the vexing problem with referrals is that you have to wait for potential customers to make that call. You really can't drive your growth. The good news? I have a solution. The system

I'll outline is a proven method for jump-starting new customer growth in a way that recognizes today's realities of finding customers.

# HSSP: Learn It, Love It

I've developed a fast-start system to grow your agency that uses referrals as a foundation, but puts you in control. I call it HSSP, which stands for "Hyper-Speed Selling Process." HSSP puts you in the driver's seat. It's designed to encourage a customer to actively seek your help and view you as a trusted professional instead of a pest.

There are four core steps to HSSP:

- Maintain an ongoing "call" list;
- Get four people to agree to meet with you each day;
- Meet with four people a day and let them know what you do;
- Follow-up with a thank-you call and gather profile information.

The combination of those four steps is more powerful than you can imagine, so let's take a look at each step in turn.

### 1. Maintain an ongoing "call" list.

You can't grow your business unless you have prospects. Prospects don't come from the phone book; those are just faceless names. Prospects have to come from people you know or have a common affiliation with. You have to build a prospect list. You have to create it through church affiliations, club affiliations, prior employment, referrals from friends and family, and so on. Your ultimate goal is to maintain a prospect list built on personal connections so that you're not just some faceless stranger. No matter where your list comes from, it's important that you carry your prospect list at all times.

## 2. Get four people to agree to meet with you each day.

Your goal is to contact people on your prospect list to obtain four introductory appointments each day. No matter how many calls it takes, you need to meet with four prospective clients every day. The purpose of your initial call *isn't* to make a sales pitch. Even the purpose of the meeting itself isn't to sell. It's merely to shake hands with potential customers, give them business cards and/or agency brochures, and have them connect your face with the sound of your voice. Your call to set up introductory appointments should go like this:

"Hello, this is [your name] with [insurance company]. I know you from [church, family friend, etc.] and I'm not calling today because I have any reason to believe that you're in the market to change agents or insurance companies. I'm calling because our studies show that people prefer to do business with people they know and trust. With that in mind, I'd like to set up a time to meet with you and introduce myself as a [insurance company] agent so that the next time you consider changing agents or companies you'll think of me first. I'll only need five minutes. What would be a good day to introduce myself to you, Monday or Tuesday? 11 a.m. or 4 p.m.?"

Making calls to set up introductory appointments is not like X-dating strangers off a purchased list because *every person on your prospect list comes from people you know.* They're referrals, or associated with a group you're affiliated with. The people on your list can be considered "warm" prospects because you obtained their phone numbers from friends, associates, or fellow club members. That personal connection makes a huge difference.

### 3. Meet with four people a day and let them know what you do.

The intent of your first meeting with a potential customer isn't to make a sale. It's merely an opportunity for you to get to know the prospect and for the prospect to get to know you. Here's the kind of greeting that works well for your face-to-face meeting:

"(Prospect name), I just wanted to introduce myself personally, give you a business card and an agency brochure, and shake your hand. If at any time in the future you consider changing agents or insurance companies, hopefully you'll think of me first. It's a pleasure to meet you. Thank you for your time and courtesy."

Leave immediately and go on to your next appointment.

Your prospect will be pleasantly surprised. Not only didn't you try to sell anything when you made the initial contact by phone, but even now, in person, you didn't try to sell anything. You didn't waste his or her valuable time. It was a quick in and out—*exactly what you promised it would be when you first contacted your prospect on the phone*. For your prospect, it's probably the first time he or she dealt with a sales person who didn't try to push a product. For you, it's the first step in building a relationship.

### 4. Follow up with a thank-you call and gather profile information.

At this point you've acquired some basic information on your prospect: name, address, telephone number, and occupation. Mark your calendar to give your potential customer a call the next day. The dialogue should go something like this:

"Hi [prospect name]. This is [your name] from [insurance company]. I just wanted to call to thank you for the courtesy you showed me yesterday. I gave you my word that I would not turn that meeting into a selling interview and, as you can see, I am a man/woman of my word. I know that at this time you're not in the market to change agents or insurance companies, but at some time in the future, most people in your position have a need for trusted advice in the areas of insurance and financial services. With your permission I'd like to take a few minutes to set up a client profile so that when you call me, I'm able to help you in the most efficient and professional manner possible. This will only take a minute."

Ask the questions and fill out the COPS form. Then thank your prospect for his or her time and say that you'll occasionally be in touch. It's human nature for people to respond positively when someone shows a genuine interest in them. You have now taken the necessary steps to continue building a relationship with your prospect.

You also have vital information on this prospect to add to your database. The beauty of the HSSP system is how quickly it multiples. Do the math. Four introductions per day multiplied by five days a week equals 20 every week. Each of your prospects probably has 10 insurance or financial services products that they purchase for his or her household. Multiply 20 x 10 = 200. Think of it! That's 200 potential product sales, and all as a result of working the HSSP system *for just one week*. Stay with it and in a year's time, you're looking at the possibility of 10,400 product placements—not a one of them from the agony of traditional cold calling, which as mentioned earlier also carries the potential risk of violating "do not call" lists.

Relationships are built on trust. My philosophy is, "I'll sell to you when you're ready to buy." The HSSP system is structured on the concept of keeping in touch to say hello and inquire about the well-being of the prospect, and doing so at the right time. It may take three to five calls to hit the timing just right, but with your retooled database and retooled staff, you're way ahead of the competition in making that happen.

# Trigger Points

So what's the next point of contact? Look for those golden trigger points. It could be when a prospect's auto insurance is due to renew, a homeowners policy is due to renew, or a daughter's 16th birthday is coming up. You'll be able to identify many of those trigger points from information you obtained from clients when you filled out the COPS form with them. For optimum results schedule a call 20 days before any given policy is due to renew. The prospect will have already received his or her renewal notice, probably hasn't actually paid it yet, and may be open to hearing what you have to offer. It's also likely your prospect has talked with you more times in the past six months than he has in the many years he's done business with his existing agent. Notice that you're not cramming anything down anyone's throat. Instead, your prospect is asking you for advice and counsel on filling his insurance needs.

## EASY, PLEASANT, AND PRODUCTIVE

*Because I've come to rely on HSSP, walking into a business on my way to lunch to introduce myself and my agency is not just easy, but also the best part of what I do. In fact, I can't tell you how many times people have tried to stop me as I'm leaving, asking me to help them with their insurance. I'm confident that's because I didn't come in to push a product on them. For them, it's a total surprise. My comeback line is always, "I didn't come to sell you anything."*

*That's the beauty of HSSP. Once people know you're not there just to make sales, they're more open to giving you information that can be used later when it is appropriate to sell. HSSP speeds up the whole relationship process.*

The HSSP system will work for you if you do it consistently. Its style of marketing will reap rewards well beyond more traditional methods, because it's based on relationships—what I've talked about since the first chapter. You'll be able to quantify your success, and justify your time and efforts because of the excellent returns.

# Chapter Highlights

— Forget cold calling and traditional X-dating. Build your agency fast by integrating the Hyper-Speed Selling Process system into your everyday workflow. It's a non-threatening approach that fuels enduring customer relationships.

— Launch HSSP by assembling a call list based on referrals and your own contacts, then follow through by setting four introductory appointments each day, brief visits, and day-after thank-you calls.

— Every introductory call gives you new prospect information. Now get your prospects to actively seek your advice and counsel by making use of trigger points that will keep your name in front of them as a trusted professional and friend.

— The math speaks volumes: A mere four introductory HSSP calls a day translates into the potential for 200 new product sales each week!

— The key to marketing is consistency. HSSP is inherently simple, and if you follow through it will work for you.

# ADD VALUE WITH FINANCIAL SERVICES PRODUCTS

# CHAPTER TWELVE

Tonight, many of your customers won't be able to fall asleep. They'll be thinking about some sort of money issue. Whether it's deciding to refinance a mortgage, worrying about whether they'll outlive their retirement savings or how they're going to finance their children's college educations, your customers know they need help. Unfortunately, because their lives are so busy they take a scattershot approach to resolving their money worries. They know they need help, yet for most, no one is offering any. That's because the financial services industry isn't built around a customer's needs. It's built around product—a structure created by federal laws that were passed to protect individual investors after the Great Depression. Even though many of those laws have been repealed, the product-focused industry silos stubbornly persist today.

Does it really matter? Absolutely. The existing structure has created an impersonal product-peddler culture in each industry, and no one is looking out for all the needs of customers. The banker only cares about getting a customer's bank account and loan business. The stockbroker or financial planner only goes after his investments. The product-peddler orientation is an anti-customer business model of the worst sort, and you need only to consider your own experiences to know how true that is. Look at banking. In order to cut costs and improve the bottom line, banks built ATMs, which reduced their contact with you. And if you invested with one of the big stock brokerage firms, you probably received a form letter from your broker—not even a telephone call— telling you that your account has been assigned to a call center. No wonder the average guy is thwarted when he tries to get a grip on his own financial affairs.

Sadly, we've been just as guilty of using an impersonal business model as other industries. In our business, the prevailing focus has long been stuck on policies in force instead of customers in force. In the process, we've inadvertently trained our customers to give us as little information about themselves as possible. They fudge the truth about the miles they drive to work. They under-report their assets in order to reduce their limits of liability. They describe their auto use as pleasure instead of business. Is this any way to deepen a relationship? It's not.

## The Opportunity

With the repeal of the Depression Era laws that segregated financial services sales by products, you're no longer limited to just selling insurance. You can broaden your product offerings in order to serve all of your customers' financial needs, and in the process transition from a product peddler to someone they can trust to help them manage their financial affairs.

Look, we all know that the big securities firms cater to clients who have hundreds of thousands of dollars to invest or who actively trade securities on the Internet. In the end, is anybody really out there for Middle America? Yes. You are—and Middle America is big.

Skeptical? Don't be. Over the last several chapters I've detailed a system that enables you to prosper in these changing times. I've explained an optimal method to re-engineer your agency into a specialist agency. I've also described how to maximize your customer relationships. But maybe you're still holding back. Maybe your doubts are driven by the perceived additional cost of hiring more staff. Maybe it's just the fear of changing the way you do business. But offering financial services products creates a dialogue that will enhance your own bottom line and enable you to help your customers sleep at night. I'll show you why, and how to make it happen.

## From Product Peddler to Trusted Financial Professional

Many people save. They just don't save consistently because they either have no plan at all, or no one to keep them in line with whatever plan they may have cobbled together. They believe they're saving if they set aside money in a bank account with a plan to invest those funds when their balance is "big enough." Unfortunately, as the balance grows they become paralyzed by the size of their account. They don't want to make a mistake. So they make an even bigger mistake by keeping their money in their bank account. Every month the value of their savings depreciates because the interest paid on a savings account in a bank is typically lower than the inflation rate.

The same story plays out with people's employer-based savings programs, such as 401(k)s. Most people don't transfer their accounts when they leave their jobs. Usually it's because they look at the balance; it's large, so they want to wait until they know exactly where to put it. The problem is that many of those 401(k) plans invest in the stock of the sponsoring company. Even though they've left that company their 401(k) balance will typically have a very high percentage invested in the company's stock. Now they're vulnerable because their balance is not diversified.

People don't know what to do or who to turn to for help. They're not looking for complicated strategies. They just want someone to assist them in staying focused on achieving their financial goals. This need holds true in a good or bad economy. In a good economy, people want to make sure their investments earn the returns they read about. But there are usually too many choices, which holds them back. In a bad economy they read about all of the losses people are incurring and they worry that their investments will be lost if they change anything. In either situation they need someone to assist them.

Once you commit to offering financial services products, you'll see a positive shift in your relationships with your customers. If you think not, then try this the next time you're at a party and people ask you what you do. Tell them you're a P&C agent. They'll probably nod and change the subject. If you're unlucky, you'll have to endure a story about a bad claims experience they've had. You've probably already encountered all of that. But now imagine the reaction you'd get if you said you're in the financial services business and that you help people manage all of their financial affairs. People would fire questions at you about the stock market, the best products to invest in, your investment approach, and other matters related to saving. They'd probably tell you about their good and bad investments. I guarantee your "job description" would be a conversation-starter instead of a conversation-stopper.

The point is, when you start selling financial services products you'll get the kind of positive feedback you've probably only dreamed about. Your customers will look at you differently, because you're no longer the "insurance guy." You're their local, trusted financial professional!

# You're Not a Stock Jock—Don't Try to Be

Many P&C agents believe they're ill-equipped to offer financial services, especially investment products. They think they need to be investment gurus to be of legitimate help to their customers. But they're wrong. Sure, if you turn on the television or open a magazine, you'll see all these impressively credentialed people offering up the investment idea of the day. It's because investment "pros" market on the "return" they'll get for you. It's a one-size-fits-all mentality, and the only way they can attract business. Remember, these people don't have customers. Their game plan is to throw everything and anything at the wall to see what'll stick. But you do have customers. That opens the door to an entirely different method, one I call the insurance-based approach to investing.

## EXTENDING YOUR RELATIONSHIPS

The insurance-based approach to investing plays off of your existing relationships with your customers. Don't forget, they already accept you as their insurance advisor. All you're doing is extending your relationship, but still within the context of what you already do—protecting people's assets. Since you're already safeguarding their most important current assets, you're simply moving yourself into the logical position of helping them protect their future as well. For example, when it comes to retirement, people are most concerned that they won't have enough money saved. You can help them. While investment pros are hunting for the best returns and talking about P/E ratios, betas of risk, and using other terminology that most of us don't understand, you can be sitting down with your customers and talking about what they do know—they have to save so they can afford to retire.

The insurance-based approach isn't just about how you position what you do with respect to investing. It's also how you seize the opportunity with your clients. The investment pros have no reason to talk to a client, so they use fancy language no one understands or they mail out charts showing their past investing performance to try to attract customers. You don't have to do that. Every day you have customers calling you. All you have to do is leverage those incoming calls. Have your staff mention to customers who call that you can now help them save for retirement or fund their children's college education. If even one person a day agrees to an appointment and if just one of the appointments translates into a sale, you will average a sale per week!

Start your discussion with a customer by focusing on his or her limits of liability. It will make you comfortable because it's something you're familiar with. But more importantly it's a natural point to start talking about a customer's assets. After all, how can you choose the appropriate limits of liability if you don't know about all of the existing assets that must be protected? With your current customers a discussion about limits of liability arises during annual reviews and whenever there is a policy change. Once those customers disclose their assets, you now have a place to start, using an opener as simple as, "Are you comfortable with your savings plan? I can now help you save for retirement."

## FINDING $300,000
## I NEVER KNEW EXISTED

*My in-house financial services registered representative was given a lead I never knew existed. I had done business with a client and friend for over 15 years. Every time we met to do a review I casually asked him about life insurance and accumulation. He always told me that there wasn't much to worry about in that area. I never delved any further. But one day one of my account executives was doing some service work for this same gentleman. The account executive probed more deeply and asked more questions in talking to him. In the process, together they uncovered a financial services opportunity in excess of $300,000. The account executive introduced the client to our registered financial services representative, thereby opening up an opportunity to roll the money into an account handled in-house. It was the same client and it was the same money that had always been there! It just took a new approach when talking with the client. Everybody* *wins in a case like this. The client has one place to go for all his or her insurance and financial services. The agency wins because it forges a deeper relationship, better retention and the trust of a friend and client.*

Getting new customers to open up about their financial affairs is just as easy as it is with your current clients. As you're filling out insurance applications for them, you'll have to choose appropriate limits of liability. Make sure you get all of the information about their assets, including their savings at that time. You want to ask about their bank accounts and if they have any IRA accounts—existing or rollover. You want to ask about any brokerage accounts to see if they have stocks, bonds, or mutual funds. You want to ask if they have any employer-sponsored savings plans, such as a 401(k). You also want to ask if they have any money from those plans still residing with their former employer. Your quest for information in context of their insurance coverage is a natural extension of what you already do. Typically, your customers will be receptive to your questions. In fact, you'll impress them with your thoroughness. But most importantly, starting a conversation based on your customers' limits of liability creates the opportunity to talk about their financial affairs in a natural way that's well within their comfort level.

# Focus on Products Everyone Needs

What do I mean when I say start selling financial services products? I mean the basics: bank accounts, loans, CDs, mutual funds, college saving plans (also known as 529 Plans), variable products, and retirement plans. People's financial affairs include a bank account to pay their bills and get cash, credit card debt, and a mortgage. Future needs include saving for retirement, funding a child's college education, and leaving money to their children. Let's take each need separately to highlight the appropriate product offerings:

## BANKING AND LOAN PRODUCTS

These are great products to offer because they open the door to a discussion of the customer's complete financial affairs. Demand deposit accounts (a.k.a. checking and savings accounts) are the low-hanging fruit. Ask your clients if they have an "emergency" money fund. Most will say they keep extra money in a checking account. However, when you dig you'll probably discover that they don't even have enough money to cover one month's expenses. Suggest they open an emergency account with you and deposit money there every month. After they have accumulated six months of expenses in the account, congratulate them. They now have peace of mind for the short term. You have just helped them take the first step in being able to sleep at night. It also allows you to transition to a savings plan because you can now suggest that they keep saving each month for the long term.

## RETIREMENT

Retirement is obviously a long-term goal. Help your customers invest for the long term with a mutual fund. Which mutual fund you recommend depends on the risk tolerance of the individual. Notice the word "risk." You already manage people's current risks. Now you're being asked to determine whether they're averse to risk, or willing to accept more risk for higher returns. It's just an extension of what you already do. I like to call the mutual fund the "auto insurance policy of the investment business." Most people know they have to purchase one; they just don't know which one to purchase. When saving for retirement use tax-deferred vehicles first, such as IRAs and 401(k)s. Use variable annuities once the tax-deferred products have been maxed out. Annuities are great for older clients looking to receive a fixed income on a periodic basis.

## COLLEGE

Saving for college is another long-term goal, typically 18 years. The most popular college savings vehicle today is the 529 Plan, named after a section of the Internal Revenue Code that provides tax benefits for this product. Think of 529 Plans as analogous to mutual funds with certain tax benefits and restrictions attached to them. Under the current federal tax rules, income from a 529 Plan is tax free. It's a great vehicle to use to save for college. For more information on 529 Plans, just go to one of the financial Internet sites, such as www.money.cnn.com or www.savingforcollege.com.

### INHERITANCE

What's left over when you die (if anything) goes to your beneficiaries. Naturally, most people want to leave something to their children. Dealing with inheritance issues tends to be a complicated area for very wealthy customers who want to shield their wealth from estate taxes. But for most people, it's simply about leaving enough for their beneficiaries. For most of your customers, their basic needs revolve around having a will that details who the beneficiaries will be.

## Getting Started with Financial Services

If I've done my job, you're now interested in offering financial services products. Getting started isn't tricky, and you don't have to be an MBA to make it happen. Neither do you have to worry whether what you're about to do involves smoke and mirrors. It doesn't.

Of course, you'll want to make some choices about which products to begin with. Different products have different features.

You'll also want to take stock of your customer base and see what kinds of initial services are most appropriate for your clients during your start-up phase, and which ones make sense for your own objectives. It's not like you have to do everything all at once. We all know it's easiest to eat an elephant one bite at a time.

But most importantly, if you decide to get involved with financial services products, you'll need to be committed, and you'll need to invest some time. That shouldn't worry you, because if you've read this far you've already demonstrated both, and you've shown that you have a proactive bent. So let's look at some specifics.

## Investment Products

If you're interested in offering investment products, your first task is to become affiliated with a broker/dealer. If you're an exclusive agent, your company probably already has a broker/dealer set up. Just contact your company and explain that you want to become registered to sell investment products. You'll need to fill out an application called a U-4. Then you'll have to pass a licensing exam called the Series 6 Exam, which is administered by the National Association of Securities Dealers (NASD). In most states you'll also have to take the Series 63 Exam as well. Don't take the exams lightly. You'll have to properly prepare. But if you do, you should pass the exams on the first sitting, so don't get intimidated. Both exams are multiple choice. The best way to study is to do as many multiple-choice questions from all the past exams you can find. There are several different self-study materials you can use. If you want more help, consult your broker/dealer for recommendations.

If your company doesn't have a broker/dealer set up, or if you're an independent agent, you'll have to find an independent broker/dealer. There are many independent broker/dealers around the country. Find another agent you know who already sells financial services and ask him about his broker/dealer. You can also consult industry periodicals, such as *Registered Rep.* magazine or *Investment News* to find names of independent broker/dealers. Once you've selected a broker/dealer, check with the NASD to make sure it is in good standing and ask to see the complaint file. Also, talk to other registered representatives at the firm to find out what they think of it. Most importantly, find out what special training programs your prospective broker/dealer offers for people new to the industry, and if the firm caters to P&C agents. What you want is a broker/dealer that offers excellent training and supervision of their registered representatives.

## GETTING THAT FIRST INVESTMENT PRODUCT SALE

Most P&C agents perceive that selling investment products is difficult. It's not. It's just that Wall Street has made investing sound so complicated that most of us don't see ourselves as the investment gurus we think we need to be. But as I said earlier, don't be trapped into thinking that you have to be an investment expert. You don't. If you offer mutual funds and variable products, it's the money managers of the underlying funds or sub-accounts who have to be the experts. You just need to figure out what the customer wants and then pick the appropriate product.

So how do you get that first sale? Start with yourself! If you remember back to when you first started selling P&C products, it wasn't the product knowledge that you were worried about. It was knowing how to fill out the auto or homeowners insurance applications so you wouldn't look foolish in front of your client. It's the same with investment products. To get comfortable, sell yourself your first investment product. Fill out the paperwork yourself. Learn by doing.

Don't try to be an expert in all the products. Focus on one specific area and become comfortable with it. I recommend you start with IRAs. You probably have one yourself or know enough about them just from what you read in the newspaper. But it's a great product to start with because most everyone should have one.

IRAs are easy to set up. With a maximum annual contribution relatively small at $4,000 and an additional "catch-up" contribution allowed for qualifying individuals over the age of 50, IRAs are also generally quite attractive to customers. You only have to determine which mutual fund to choose for the customer. Again, this is not as complicated as it sounds. All you need to know about your customer is what his risk tolerance is. Typically, the mutual fund application has a risk tolerance questionnaire. Once you determine a customer's risk tolerance, you merely have to find the mutual fund that best matches the customer's risk tolerance. Each mutual fund family has publications that divide their mutual funds by risk level. If this sounds similar to "rating" a P&C customer, you're right. It is.

## Life's Never Been Easier

One of the pleasant discoveries you'll make when you start marketing financial services products is how easy it is to sell life insurance to your customers. Once again, the positioning and ultimate sale will occur from an insurance-based approach. When you discuss setting up a bank account to hold emergency funds, you're protecting your customers if they lose their jobs or something unforeseen happens where they need quick access to cash.

When you discuss investing with someone, what you are really talking about is protecting them from running out of money if they live a long life. Investing is based on the principle of saving now so you can have money in the future to fund the retirement for you and your spouse, or college for your kids. But what if you die too soon? If you don't have "die too soon" protection, your financial goals will be destroyed. In this context, life insurance becomes an anchor for every financial plan. It's a natural outgrowth of the investment process. More importantly, by segueing into financial services products, life sales will become a natural transition for you.

## DON'T JUST FISH FOR WHALES

*My manager, Jay Green, was fond of telling me, "Don't go out fishing only for whales." In fact, when I started my agency in 1983 he advised that I "go fishing for everything." He also said, "If you put enough lines in the water, you are going to catch something—and usually more than one of something." But Jay didn't stop there. He added, "If you get your lines out there enough, you are going to catch a few whales."*

*In today's terms that means we must look at our book of business as an opportunity to sell financial services to each of our clients. Don't go after just the folks who look like they have a lot of money. Get a system that helps you "touch" every household in which you do business. With enough lines in the water we're all bound to hit a few whales. In the meantime, the service we provide, no matter how small the transaction, will be of mutual benefit to our clients and our agencies.*

# Chapter Highlights

— Mr. and Mrs. Middle America are screaming for help in sorting out their financial affairs and making sure they have what they need when they need it. Be there for them! Transition from being a product peddler to becoming a trusted financial professional.

— Offering financial services is ideally suited for insurance agents. Your customers already rely on you for insurance advice. All you have to do is extend your relationship.

— Don't get hung up on what to offer. Focus on providing the financial products you already know everyone needs: bank accounts, loans, CDs, mutual funds, college saving plans, variable products, and retirement plans.

— Do your homework. Get yourself affiliated with a broker/ dealer to get started, and invest some time in studying for any necessary exams. Practice your new skills by selling your first financial product to yourself.

— Plan for your own retirement first! The income potential from offering financial services products is excellent.

# A CALL TO ARMS
## CHAPTER THIRTEEN

I'm absolutely convinced that changes in the past few years in the insurance and financial services marketplace have opened the door to the greatest opportunity I've seen in years. Many agents I've worked with were initially reluctant to make the transitions that today's market demands. What they discovered, however, is that once they got past the fear of change, actually making the changes was easy. This book is a road map to building a great agency. You must believe in your heart of hearts that you can guide your agency to bring it there. That's what *Profit from Change* is all about. My goal is to help you be more successful. Period. Agents all across America are on the pathway to change, one step at a time. You can do it too!

## Start a Crusade

I've worked with some agents who have taken their agencies to the next level by launching a personal crusade to build high-quality/high-density households focused on client relationships. They started their crusade by identifying 10 target households with the means and need for additional products, using the systems detailed in this book. Target households are easy to identify using the Relationship Focused Agency (RFA) system described in

Chapter Nine.

Picture yourself as one of those crusading agents. Using the principles in this book, imagine that you've identified your own 10 target households. Now imagine that among your target households, you have a client who lives in an excellent neighborhood, and that your agency already insures his family's three cars and home. You reflect on the next step, asking yourself about the likelihood that your client's family needs an umbrella policy and has other possessions to insure. It doesn't take you long to come up with an answer. The probability is excellent. But you don't stop there, because you're a proactive thinker now. You've taken measures to retool your agency for an unprecedented advantage, and you're on a roll! So your thoughts have already taken you to the next logical step in identifying the family as a good prospect for life insurance and financial services. You launch a quest to round out the household with more products. Systematically, you personally call each of your remaining targets to schedule a meeting, a lunch, a golf outing—whatever it takes to create an opportunity to build a closer relationship with every client. As each of your target households is rounded out, you add another target household to your list. Along the way? You've learned what those 10 original crusaders did: It really is that easy to begin transforming your agency.

# CRUSADING WITH ACCOUNTABILITY

While you're crusading to build your agency, you wear several hats. For that matter, the first one or two employees you hire also have several areas of responsibility. That's all right. A lot of people are receptive to taking responsibility, and the best of them are downright proud to be held accountable. Indeed, you'll witness your employees flourish as your agency grows.

Successful business owners understand that accountability is an essential ingredient in their success. They do their best to choose the most talented staff members they can find, recruiting people to whom they feel comfortable delegating responsibility. But at the end of the day, ultimate accountability for what happens in your agency rests solely with you. If you're still a practitioner who has one or no employees, it will be your responsibility to devote time each day to one of the most valuable business assets you'll ever have—the information in your database.

Information is the heart and soul of your business. It's your most powerful tool for building relationships that matter with your customers. You must keep that information current on a daily basis, and it has to grow in order to move your agency forward. Whether it's you inputting that information or someone else, make sure it happens. Crusading with old or incomplete information isn't crusading at all. At best, it's marching in place.

## FASTEN YOUR SEATBELTS
## AND ENJOY THE RIDE

Nobody can dispute the turbulent changes that have swept the insurance and financial services industries. They've made for a wild ride, indeed. But I'm reminded of a story that speaks volumes about why we do what we do, and how we can not only weather change, but turn it to our benefit.

### IT'S NOT ABOUT THE FOOD

*A friend and I were on the road one day looking for a place to eat lunch. It was almost three o'clock when we spotted a tiny restaurant on the corner of a busy street. It was called Pita Kitchen and we surmised that if it was crowded at this time of day it must be a pretty good place to eat. We went inside and both ordered a couple of chicken pitas and sat down at one of the restaurant's four tables. At best, the restaurant was 200 square feet, but it was neat and clean, and it bustled with activity.*

*We overheard a conversation between one of the patrons and the owner. The patron, obviously a regular, was encouraging the owner to open another location. The owner didn't disagree with the idea, but said he had to wait to find the right employ-*

*ees. The patron suggested running a general ad in the newspaper.*

*That's when the owner looked up and replied, "I can't do that! If I open another restaurant with the wrong people, I would go out of business. My customers want to see me, they expect me to kibitz with them and talk to them. I have to find and train people who can develop that same kind of relationship. It's the ambiance of this place that makes it popular and I have to hire somebody who will be able to create that ambiance."*

*Then he made a statement that was just as profound for our business as well. He said, "It's not about the food; the food has to be good for any restaurant to survive. It's definitely not the surroundings. This is a little hole in the wall. It's about the fact that when people walk in here they feel like they have a relationship with me and my employees. The key to the success of my business, and I believe any business, is cultivating that customer relationship. If I do that, I know my customers will return again and again."*

The restaurant owner had it right. In the commodity world of fast food, hamburgers and hotdogs, the only way the local guy can distinguish himself and not just survive but prosper, is to do what the big guys can't—cultivate a relationship with customers. No matter what size agency you have it still doesn't come close to being as big as the direct writers. The only way you're going to be able to prosper in these incredible, changing times is to offer your customers something they can't get anywhere else. And that's the knowledge that they can rely on someone local to get a question answered or resolve a problem. That someone is an individual with whom they have a trusting relationship. That someone is you, and that relationship is your competitive advantage. That's what you need to focus on every day to thrive.

## Sleep Well—Distribution Is Still the Key

How many of you have heard, "Distribution is the key?" That statement was true 50 years ago, and it's still true today. Distribution will always be the key—and you are the key ingredient of that distribution.

Big companies will always be exploring more efficient ways to do things. They'll always look at ways to reduce costs. The reason why the agency-based distribution channel has survived is because of the value of the personal relationship between agent and customer. However, if you, as an insurance and financial services professional, allow yourself to become less customer focused and more commodity focused, you run a risk. If you allow the relationships you have to stagnate or dissipate, you'll diminish your value and the value of the agency-distribution channel as a whole. What you do matters! And if you adapt and change using the systems I outlined in this book, your agency will thrive.

# Some Closing Thoughts

What I've tried to do in this book is describe all of the things going on in our industry and the world around us that present incredible opportunities for you. In sharing my experience, I believe I've given you excellent systems to follow to reach new heights.

Remember, though, that moving your agency forward can't happen if you do the same things you've always done. There are far too many changes impacting our industry to risk an indifferent approach. You must adapt and change. If you follow my suggestions in doing that, I believe you'll not only survive any transition coming your way, but will profit immensely, ensuring for you and your family the wealth and the freedom to enjoy it.

Good luck on your journey. I wish you an abundance of profit from change.

# Chapter Highlights

— Over the last few years change has throttled our industry, but it's also opened doors to some of the greatest opportunities available in years. Grab them!

— Start a crusade to build high-quality/high-density households by focusing on your relationship with key customers.

— The information in your database is an essential business asset. You can assign responsibility for it to a trusted employee, but ultimately it's you who must accept accountability for keeping it current—and growing.

— The agency-based distribution channel is still paramount, but its ultimate survival is dependent on every agent's commitment to building enduring customer-focused relationships. So keep that personal touch with your customers. The "big guys" can't even begin to duplicate the advantage it gives you.

— Be an evangelist of change. When you embrace transition and adapt for the future, you'll enjoy unprecedented opportunities for growth and profit.

# EXHIBITS

**E X H I B I T   A**

Agency Evaluation Worksheet

— Annual Agency Revenue by Product Line

— Annual Agency Expenses

Learning from this Exercise

**E X H I B I T   B**

Sample Road Map to Growing Your Agency

(A View from 30,000 Feet)

**E X H I B I T   C**

Creating an Agency Playbook

# AGENCY EVALUATION WORKSHEET

Agency Name _____

Current number of employees: _____

Full-time _____    Part-time _____

Has the number of employees changed in the past 12 months?

Yes _____        No _____

Gain _____       Loss _____

Number of Policies-In-Force (PIF):        _____

Number of Policies-In-Force a year ago:   _____

PIF Growth (loss) in the past 12 months:  _____

Percentage of PIF Growth (loss):          _____

Total number of households served:        _____

Average Number of PIF per household:  _____

> Divide total PIF by number of households to determine the average number
> of policies (density) per household. (Example: 1,874 PIF divided by 900
> households = Density of 2.08)

# ANNUAL AGENCY REVENUE BY PRODUCT LINE

Divide Product Line Revenue by TOTAL Revenue to Determine Percentage

| Product Line | Annual Revenue | % of Annual Revenue | # of Policies |
|---|---|---|---|
| **INVESTMENT PRODUCTS** | | | |
| Mutual Funds | $_____ | _____ | _____ |
| Variable Annuities | $_____ | _____ | _____ |
| Fixed Annuities | $_____ | _____ | _____ |
| **LIFE PRODUCTS** | | | |
| Life Insurance | $_____ | _____ | _____ |
| Long-Term Care | $_____ | _____ | _____ |
| Disability | $_____ | _____ | _____ |
| **P&C INSURANCE** | | | |
| Auto | $_____ | _____ | _____ |
| RVs, Boats | $_____ | _____ | _____ |
| Motorcycles | $_____ | _____ | _____ |
| Antique auto | $_____ | _____ | _____ |
| Fire | $_____ | _____ | _____ |
| Umbrellas | $_____ | _____ | _____ |
| **COMMERCIAL INSURANCE** | | | |
| Truck | $_____ | _____ | _____ |
| Workers comp | $_____ | _____ | _____ |
| Other: | | | |
| _____ | $_____ | _____ | _____ |

TOTAL REVENUE $_____

Compare your Total Revenue with revenue a year ago:

Increase of $ _____ or decrease of $_____

# ANNUAL AGENCY EXPENSES

| | |
|---|---|
| Staff Payroll | $_____ |
| Agent Draw/Salary | $_____ |
| Property Payments/Rent | $_____ |
| Utilities | $_____ |
| Telephone | $_____ |
| Auto Expense | $_____ |
| Technology Expense | $_____ |
| Continuing Education | $_____ |
| Professional Fees | $_____ |
| Marketing Expense* | $_____ |
| Office Supplies | $_____ |
| Postage | $_____ |
| Dues & Subscriptions | $_____ |
| Business Entertainment | $_____ |
| Business Travel | $_____ |
| Income Tax | $_____ |
| Payroll Tax | $_____ |
| Other Taxes | $_____ |
| Insurance | |
|    Workers Comp. | $_____ |
|    Errors & Omissions | $_____ |
|    Liability Contents Package | $_____ |
|    Auto Insurance | $_____ |
|    Group Health Insurance | $_____ |
|    Other Insurance | $_____ |
| Business Debt Expense | $_____ |
| Other Business Expense | $_____ |
| TOTAL EXPENSE | $_____ |

THE BOTTOM LINE

| | |
|---|---|
| Total Revenue | $_____ |
| Total Expense (subtract) | $_____ |
| Net Profit (Loss) | $_____ |
| As a Percentage of Revenue: | _____% |

*(Include external marketing expense: advertising, brochures, presentation materials, entertainment, etc. Internal marketing expense typically falls within other categories.)

# LEARNING FROM THIS EXERCISE

1. Are product sales balanced or would selling more or less of a particular product line increase agency profits?

2. For the agency to grow, what needs to change?
   List in order of importance:

   a. _____  Estimated cost: $_____

   b. _____  Estimated cost: $_____

   c. _____  Estimated cost: $_____

3. Can the most important changes be tackled at the same time?
   Yes _____  No _____

Here's a typical example of an agency grossing $100,000 per year:

|  | **Annual Revenue** | **% of Annual Revenue** |
|---|---|---|
| Auto | $49,500 | 49.5% |
| Fire | 28,000 | 28% |
| Life | 9,000 | 9% |
| Commercial | 7,300 | 7.3% |
| Financial Services | 3,200 | 3.2% |
| Other | 3,000 | 3% |
| **Gross** | **$100,000** | **100%** |

As you can see in this example, there are lots of eggs in the auto basket, which as we all know, is expensive in terms of service time.

Now let's play, "what if." What if auto represented only 32 percent of this agency's book of business and more staff time was devoted to selling life, fire, and umbrellas? What if the agent's time were freed up to focus on selling financial services? Let's see what happens to the book of business balance and projected revenue in just one year.

|  | Annual Revenue | % of Annual Revenue |
| --- | --- | --- |
| Auto | $40,000 | 32.4% |
| Fire | 40,000 | 32.5% |
| Life | 18,000 | 14.6% |
| Financial Services | 10,000 | 8.1% |
| Commercial | 7,300 | 5.9% |
| Umbrella | 5,000 | 4.0% |
| Other | 3,000 | 2.6% |
| **Gross** | **$123,300** | **100%** |

There is $23,300 in agency growth with no additional expense, thus the increase falls directly to the bottom line. And all you did was make minor adjustments to product-line focus. Imagine how dramatic the bottom-line results could be if you added staff and offered more products to your existing customer base.

# SAMPLE ROAD MAP TO GROWING YOUR AGENCY (A View from 30,000 Feet)

Your road map—or business plan—should be thoughtful and complete, but not complicated. Use the following development points to make sure you include the most important elements that will guide your agency's growth. For expanded discussion on each element and the full scope of a road map, please take another look at Chapter Five.

## 1) Develop an Agency Mission Statement

Develop a mission statement, or philosophy, that reflects the personality of your agency. It should showcase your values, goals and vision for operating your business. Include a statement about the unique qualities of your agency, the level of service a customer can expect, and so on. Your mission statement doesn't have to be long, but it should be something you can proudly share with your staff and clients.

## 2) Financial Goals Based on Product Lines

Determine which product lines you will sell. Establish a financial goal for each product line, and write down your overall projections.

Year 1   $_____

Year 2   $_____

Year 3   $_____

### 3) Write a specific agency playbook

Your agency playbook should spell out the steps you will take to achieve the broader goals you set in your road map. The following examples show you the kinds of focus areas you'll want to include:

*Example 1:* Establish relationships with three mortgage brokers to provide leads for homeowners insurance.

*Example 2:* Review my customer base to ferret out prospects for financial services products.

*Example 3:* Begin a list of 100 life prospects and set an appointment with each one—a life appointment every day for 100 days.

### 4) Staff Planning

Determine when you will add staff and which department you will create first. Plan for when you add the next staff person. Will your present office space accommodate additional staff, or will you need to arrange for increased space?

### 5) Periodic Review of Map

After your road map has been in action for three months, review it to make sure you are still on target. Make any necessary adjustments and continue to review your plan often.

EXHIBIT | C

# CREATING AN AGENCY PLAYBOOK

You wouldn't expect the coach of an NFL team to challenge an opponent without having a playbook. It's a detailed plan of how the team will approach the game. Your business is no different. Earlier you analyzed your business and wrote a road map outlining your goals and vision for the future. Now it's time to create detailed action plans, your personal agency playbook. Your playbook is your tactical plan—the action steps that will help you focus on the important things first, then initiate the changes necessary in your agency to deliver a win. And just like the NFL coach, it's important to share the playbook with your employees so that everyone playing on the team is headed toward the same goal post.

### *Example:*

My agency currently serves _____ households with an average household penetration of _____ percent. My primary focus (as a small agency) is to grow the agency.

Within the next three years, I will double the number of households that we currently serve and place at least three products in each household.

# YEAR 1

❑ I will get my Series 6 and 63 licenses.

❑ I will gain my Life Underwriters Training Council (LUTC) certification.

❑ I will set four new introduction appointments every day for a year.

❑ I will set a minimum of three life appointments per day for a year.

❑ I will qualify for my company's achievement club.

❑ Marketing strategy: Utilize a "new movers" list and our ACR to market auto, renters, and homeowners insurance to people who have recently moved to our marketing area.

❑ Agency revenue goal: $ _____

# YEAR 2

❑ I will set a minimum of three life appointments per day.

❑ I will set a minimum of three financial services appointments per day.

❑ I will set four new introduction appointments every day for 90 days.

❑ By the end of the year I will employ a staff of four people:
   1 Agency Producer (auto and fire)
   2 CSRs (auto and fire)
   1 Agency Contact Representative (ACR)

❑ I will provide superior training for new hires using all resources available

❑ I will qualify for my company's achievement club.

❑ I will begin setting up departments within the agency.

❑ I will gain two new commercial clients per month.

❑ Marketing strategy: Develop an attractive agency brochure to mail to the "new movers" list. Other targets: homeowners in new development being built in our neighborhood.

❑ Agency revenue goal: $ _____

# YEAR 3

❑  I will move agency to larger office.

❑  I will hire an additional Agency Producer for life department.

❑  I will hire a full-time receptionist/marketing assistant.

❑  I will set a minimum of three life appointments per day.

❑  I will set a minimum of three financial services appointments
      per day.

❑  Each AP will set four new introduction appointments every day.

❑  I will qualify for my company's top achievement award.

❑  I will continue the process of departmentalizing the agency.

❑  I will gain three new commercial clients per month.

❑  Agency revenue goal: $ _____

In order to reach these goals we must maintain a _____% Customer
Loyalty Ratio and a ___% Life Lapse Ratio.

# BENCHMARK GOALS

## YEAR ONE

- ❏ Agency income        $_____
- ❏ No. of households served      _____
- ❏ Cumulative PIF      _____
- ❏ Qualify for Achievement Club
- ❏ Make financial services products 5 percent of our policy sales
- ❏ Achieve life bonus every quarter

## YEAR TWO

- ❏ Agency income        $_____
- ❏ No. of households served      _____
- ❏ Cumulative PIF      _____
- ❏ Qualify for Achievement Club
- ❏ Make financial services products 10 percent of our policy sales
- ❏ Achieve life bonus every quarter
- ❏ Write 12 commercial accounts

## YEAR THREE

- ❏ Agency income        $_____
- ❏ No. of households served      _____
- ❏ Cumulative PIF      _____
- ❏ Qualify for Achievement Club
- ❏ Make financial services products 15 percent of our policy sales
- ❏ Achieve life bonus every quarter
- ❏ Write 20 commercial accounts

# PUTTING YOUR PLAYBOOK INTO ACTION

Which item has the highest priority in your playbook? Focus on first things first. Your priority may be hiring additional staff or setting a higher number of annual review appointments. Or it may be to make four introduction appointments every day. Whatever your No. 1 priority, take action on it today! Don't procrastinate. View this day as an opportunity to compete in the Super Bowl. Go into the game with an overall plan supported by the details to make it work and be successful. And remember, it may be a series of small changes that you will be making. Whether the changes are big or small, it doesn't matter. What matters is that you get into the game!

PROFIT FROM CHANGE

# EXHIBITS

APPENDIX TWO

## EXHIBIT A

Household Update Sheet

# HOUSEHOLD UPDATE SHEET

Name _____

Address _____

City/State/Zip _____

Home Phone _____ Fax _____

Mr. Work _____ Ms. Work _____

*Request OCCUPATION for discount purposes:*

Mr. _____ Mrs. _____

Mr. Fax _____ Mrs. Fax _____

Mr. Cell _____ Ms. Cell _____

Mr. Pager _____ Ms. Pager _____

Mr. E-Mail _____ Ms. E-Mail _____

| | Currently Insured With | Expiration Date |
|---|---|---|
| Auto | | |
| Auto Loan | | |
| Boat/Jet Ski/Yacht | | |
| Motorcycle | | |
| CD's/T-Bills/401K, etc. | | |
| Classic Cars | | |
| Commercial | | |
| Disability | | |
| Health | | |
| Home/Fire/Rentals | | |
| Homeowners Warranty | | |
| Jewelry | | |
| Life | | |
| Long-Term Care | | |
| Vehicle Breakdown Ins. | | |
| Rec. Vehicle | | |
| Mutual Funds | | |
| Mortgage Protection | | |
| Umbrella | | |

# EXHIBITS

## EXHIBIT A

Group A Gap Analysis, Part 1

Group A Gap Analysis, Part 2—What's Missing?

## EXHIBIT B

Six Marketing Letters

— Auto, No Fire

— Fire, No Auto

— Auto/Fire, No Life

— Auto/Fire, No Umbrella

— Introducing Financial Services

— Long-Term Care

## EXHIBIT C

Account Plan Checklist

## EXHIBIT D

Employee Evaluation Form

## EXHIBIT E

COPS—Customer Opportunity Profile System

# GROUP A GAP ANALYSIS, PART 1

| Household Name | # of Policies |
|---|---|
| _____ | 6 |
| _____ | 6 |
| | |
| _____ | 5 |
| _____ | 5 |
| _____ | 5 |
| | |
| _____ | 4 |
| _____ | 4 |
| _____ | 4 |
| _____ | 4 |
| | |
| _____ | 3 |
| _____ | 3 |
| _____ | 3 |
| _____ | 3 |
| _____ | 3 |
| _____ | 3 |
| _____ | 3 |
| | |
| _____ | 2 |
| _____ | 2 |
| _____ | 2 |
| _____ | 2 |
| _____ | 2 |
| _____ | 2 |
| _____ | 2 |
| _____ | 2 |
| _____ | 2 |
| _____ | 2 |
| _____ | 2 |

# GROUP A GAP ANALYSIS, PART 2—WHAT'S MISSING?

| Household Name | # of Policies | Currently Insured | What's Missing? |
|---|---|---|---|
| _____ | 4 | auto, auto loan, boat, fire | financial services, life |
| _____ | 4 | auto, auto loan, boat, fire | financial services, life |
| _____ | 4 | auto, auto loan, boat, fire | financial services, life |
| _____ | 4 | auto, auto loan, boat, fire | financial services, life |
| _____ | 3 | auto, fire, life | umbrella |
| _____ | 3 | auto, fire, life, | umbrella |
| _____ | 3 | auto, fire, life | umbrella |
| _____ | 3 | auto, fire, umbrella | life |
| _____ | 3 | auto, fire, umbrella | life |
| _____ | 3 | auto, fire, umbrella | life |
| _____ | 3 | auto, fire, umbrella | life |
| _____ | 2 | auto, fire | life, umbrella |
| _____ | 2 | auto, fire | life, umbrella |
| _____ | 2 | auto, fire | life, umbrella |
| _____ | 2 | auto, fire | life, umbrella |
| _____ | 2 | auto, life | fire, umbrella |
| _____ | 2 | auto, life | fire, umbrella |
| _____ | 2 | auto, life | fire, umbrella |
| _____ | 2 | auto, life | fire, umbrella |
| _____ | 2 | fire, life | auto |
| _____ | 2 | fire, life | auto |
| _____ | 2 | fire, life | auto |

# MARKETING LETTER: AUTO, NO FIRE

**The Jack Agent Insurance and Financial Services Agency**
**1111 Agency St.**
**Everywhere, USA 99999**

Date

Mr. and Mrs. John Q. Customer
1234 Anywhere Ave.
Anytown, U.S.A. 99999

Dear John Q. Customer,

Thank you for carrying your auto insurance with [company name] and the [agency name]. We appreciate the trust you have placed in us.

In reviewing your file I noted that we do not currently carry your homeowners [renters] insurance. You may qualify for discounts by placing this coverage with our agency. Need easy monthly payments for all the insurance you place with [company name]? No problem. We can set up a payment plan that works for you.

For professional advice on any insurance need, please call me today at [agency telephone number]. We can take care of your insurance and financial services needs ranging from auto, life, homeowners, and recreational vehicles, and we offer several plans to save for retirement.

Let me show you the many ways you come out ahead with [company name]. Call me! I'll be happy to sit down with you personally and provide a review of all your insurance and financial services needs.

Cordially,

Jack Agent

P.S. Call today to set an appointment! We could save you money that you can invest in your future instead.

# MARKETING LETTER: FIRE, NO AUTO

**The Jack Agent Insurance and Financial Services Agency**
**1111 Agency St.**
**Everywhere, USA 99999**

Date

Mr. and Mrs. John Q. Customer
1234 Anywhere Ave.
Anytown, U.S.A. 99999

Dear John Q. Customer,

Thank you for carrying your homeowners insurance with [company name] and the [agency name]. We appreciate the trust you have placed in us.

In reviewing your file I noted that we do not currently carry your auto insurance. You may qualify for discounts by placing this coverage with our agency. Need easy monthly payments for all the insurance you place with [company name]? No problem. We can set up a payment plan that works for you.

For professional advice on any insurance need, please call me today at [agency telephone number]. We can take care of your insurance and financial services needs ranging from auto, life, homeowners, and recreational vehicles, and we offer several plans to save for retirement.

Let me show you the many ways you come out ahead with [company name]. Call me! I'll be happy to sit down with you and provide a review of all your insurance and financial services needs.

Cordially,


Jack Agent

P.S. Call today to set an appointment! We could save you money that you can invest in your future instead.

# MARKETING LETTER: AUTO/FIRE, NO LIFE

**The Jack Agent Insurance and Financial Services Agency**
**1111 Agency St.**
**Everywhere, USA 99999**

Date

Mr. and Mrs. John Q. Customer
1234 Anywhere Ave.
Anytown, U.S.A.  99999

Dear John Q. Customer,

Thank you for carrying your auto and homeowners insurance with
[company name] and the [agency name]. We appreciate the trust
you have placed in us.

In reviewing your file I noted that we do not currently carry your life
insurance. While you may already have some life insurance coverage,
many people in your position have discovered that in this era of rising
real estate prices their current life coverage is no longer adequate to
protect their families.

I'll be happy to sit down with you and provide a review of all your
insurance and financial services needs. Please call me today at
[agency telephone number] to set an appointment to review this
important information.

Cordially,


Jack Agent

# MARKETING LETTER: AUTO/FIRE, NO UMBRELLA

**The Jack Agent Insurance and Financial Services Agency**
**1111 Agency St.**
**Everywhere, USA 99999**

Date

Mr. and Mrs. John Q. Customer
1234 Anywhere Ave.
Anytown, U.S.A.  99999

Dear John Q. Customer,

Thank you for carrying your auto and homeowners insurance with [company name] and the [agency name]. We appreciate the trust you have placed in us.

In reviewing your file I noted that you do not currently have umbrella coverage with our agency. Many people in your position have discovered that this liability coverage is necessary to adequately protect their assets. In addition, you may qualify for discounts by placing this coverage with our agency.

I'll be happy to sit down with you and provide a review of all your insurance and financial services needs. Please call me today at [agency telephone number] to set an appointment to review this important information.

Cordially,


Jack Agent

# MARKETING LETTER: INTRODUCING FINANCIAL SERVICES

**The Jack Agent Insurance and Financial Services Agency**
**1111 Agency St.**
**Everywhere, USA 99999**

Date

Mr. and Mrs. John Q. Customer
1234 Anywhere Ave.
Anytown, U.S.A. 99999

Dear John Q. Customer,

Over the last year I've started receiving lots of requests from clients seeking help with their investments. They are concerned that they are not saving enough for retirement, but intimidated about investing on their own. What I've realized is this is one of the most important issues facing each of my clients. I would imagine it's yours too.

It's why I decided to offer investment services as a new and important part of my agency. Specifically I want to help you develop and then execute your savings plan. It's not much different than what I already do. Today you trust me to protect your most valuable assets. It only makes sense that I help you build and protect your future assets.

I only offer basic investment products like mutual funds and variable products. I don't trade securities, invest in hedge funds or other complicated and risky investments. My approach is simple. People fail to invest properly because they have no one to keep them on the straight and narrow. No one to make sure they save every month and no one to call when the stock market tumbles.

All I ask is that you commit to invest a set amount each month and then visit with me annually to re-evaluate your investment choices.

As a valued client, I would like to set up an appointment to meet with you to discuss your savings plan. If you don't have one, I'd like to start one with you. If you do, I'd like to review it and make sure it's aligned with your long-term savings goals.

I will follow up with a phone call to schedule an appointment. I look forward to meeting with you.

Cordially,

Jack Agent

# MARKETING LETTER: LONG-TERM CARE

Target all households that include a family member in the 50- to 65-year-old range.

**The Jack Agent Insurance and Financial Services Agency
1111 Agency St.
Everywhere, USA 99999**

Date

Mr. and Mrs. John Q. Customer
1234 Anywhere Ave.
Anytown, U.S.A.  99999

Dear John Q. Customer,

A national study projects that 43 percent of those people who turned age 65 in 1990 will enter a nursing home at some time during their lifetime. This startling statistic underscores the value of having long-term care insurance protection. This coverage can also pay for at-home nursing or care received at an assisted living facility.

I'll be happy to sit down with you and review the details of [company name]'s long-term care coverage so that you can make an informed decision about whether this coverage is appropriate for you or a loved one.

Please call me today at [agency telephone number] to set an appointment to review this important information.

Cordially,


Jack Agent

# ACCOUNT PLAN CHECKLIST

| | | *I.T.Q.* | | | |
|---|---|---|---|---|---|
| *Date* | *Initial* | *Date* | *Initial* | *Date* | *Initial* |
| _____ | ____ | _____ | ____ | _____ | ____ |

### Check all items you want to include in the Account Plan for:

Customer Name _____

Company Name _____

Customer Address _____

City _____ State _____ Zip _____

Telephone (Home) _____ (Work) _____

Cell/Pager (His) _____ (Hers):_____

E-mail _____

## ACTION NEEDED                    FOLLOW -UP DATE

❏  Personal Phone Call            _____

❏  Personal Note                  _____

❏  Lunch Certificate              _____

❏  Personal Delivery of Policy    _____

❏  Make Presentation for Customer
    and/or Their Employees         _____

❏  Deliver Pie(s)                 _____

❏  Personal Note with Agency Gift _____

❏  Gift Basket                    _____

❏  Other _____     _____

## NEXT LINE OF BUSINESS FOCUS:

**PRODUCT LINE      ACTION NEEDED      FOLLOW UP DATE**

_____     _____     _____

# EMPLOYEE EVALUATION FORM

Employee name _____

Review Date: _____

Current salary: $ _____


**Attendance:**                             Excellent    Good    Average    Fair

**Overall work habits:**                    Excellent    Good    Average    Fair

**Gets along with other employees:** Excellent    Good    Average    Fair

**Customer service:**                       Excellent    Good    Average    Fair

What needs to improve:

_____

Specific recommendation to accomplish this:

_____


**Up-selling skills:**                      Excellent    Good    Average    Fair

What needs to improve:

_____

Specific recommendation to accomplish this:

_____

**Computer skills:** Excellent  Good  Average  Fair

What needs to improve:

---

Specific recommendation to accomplish this:

---

**Telephone skills:** Excellent  Good  Average  Fair

What needs to improve:

---

Specific recommendation to accomplish this:

---

**Organizational skills:** Excellent  Good  Average  Fair

What needs to improve:

---

Specific recommendation to accomplish this:

---

**Takes responsibility, follows
up without supervision:** Excellent  Good  Average  Fair

What needs to improve:

---

Specific recommendation to accomplish this:

---

**Cooperation and willingness
to learn new  skills:**     Excellent   Good   Average   Fair

What needs to improve:

_____

Specific recommendation to accomplish this:

_____

**Grooming/personal habits:**   Excellent   Good   Average   Fair

What needs to improve:

_____

Specific recommendation to accomplish this:

_____

**Salary recommendation:**     Keep the same _____

Increase by $_____

Other comments:

_____

_____

_____

_____

_____

**Next employee review:**   3 months   6 months   12 months

# CUSTOMER OPPORTUNITY PROFILE SYSTEM (COPS)

Use the COPS form to keep your staff members on a fact-finding mission every time they make contact with a customer. They can use the key phrases as prompts to get new or updated information for your database. They can use the chart to quickly note or refer to specifics about products placed with your agency—and to swing products away from the competition!

## KEY PHRASES

"I want to make sure we have the proper information in your file."

"I notice that we don't carry your _____ insurance. Who do you currently have that with? And when is that up for renewal?"

"Do you have life insurance through your company? How much coverage do you have?"

"Is your spouse also covered on that policy?"

"Do you currently have a long-term care policy?"

"Do you have an IRA or a savings plan for retirement? CDs or mutual funds?"

| Product | Notes |
|---|---|
| Auto | |
| Specialty Vehicles. (motorcycles, boats, motor homes, etc) | |
| Auto Loans | |
| Home/Fire | |
| Life | |
| Long-Term Care | |
| Financial Services | |
| Banking | |
| Other | |

Use the COPS to catch the "bad boys."

Bad Boys = customers who do not have ALL products placed with your agency. It's a crime!

| Trigger Event | X-Date | Current Carrier |
|---|---|---|
|  |  |  |
|  |  |  |
|  |  |  |
|  |  |  |
|  |  |  |
|  |  |  |
|  |  |  |
|  |  |  |
|  |  |  |

**TKS** TROY
KORSGADEN
SYSTEMS

TKSystems offers cutting-edge strategy programs for agents, support staff, field leadership, and additionally has been involved at the home office level on several nationwide roll-out programs. Led by Troy Korsgaden, long recognized as a leading expert and motivational speaker in the insurance industry, TKSystems has worked as the project lead with several large carriers to create nationwide marketing programs, agent and staff training programs, selling systems and company-to-agency communication programs. The consulting firm has also been outsourced for consulting in the areas of leading practices and best practices.

In addition to consulting work, Troy is highly sought after as a main platform speaker. He has addressed many major industry events, including the prestigious GAMA-sponsored LAMP convention in 2002.

The expertise he brings to national conventions is also available to individual businesses through seminars and workshops that are carefully tailored to each company's specific needs, venue, and forum. Indeed, Troy's services, popular with companies using multi-line distribution systems, have likewise been retained by many mono-line and life-only companies eager to enhance their prospects for growth.

TKSystems takes pride in its pioneering solutions, which have helped thousands of agents integrate new technology, CRM, innovative marketing and retention programs, and the enhanced staff specialization business model.

# ADDITIONAL PRODUCTS FROM TKS SYSTEMS

## Power Position Your Agency:
## A Guide to Insurance Agency Success

Soft Cover edition (Discount given for orders of 50 or more). Discover the keys to building a bigger, more efficient, more profitable agency. This award-winning author/agent shares his insight, experience and expertise so you can power position your agency.

### *CD-ROM*
### Power Position Your Agency: A Guide to Insurance Agency Success

The latest release in GAMA's Desktop Masters Series. Use this 9-step program to ensure the success and growth of your agency. Included is the support material to get you started—telephone scripts, forms to smooth and speed daily workflow, and job descriptions for every slot in a growing agency—and keep the momentum building.

## Building a Successful Insurance Agency:
## The Power Series [audio CD]

This Audio CD details the 4 essential steps to building a powerful agency, poised for growth and success. You will learn step by step the winning formulas that can propel your agency to a higher level of achievement.

### Specialization: The DNA of Agency Transformation [audio CD]

Create a collaboration of experts in order to compete and grow your agency into the future. Includes the building blocks to creating a Specialist Agency.

### Agent Contact Representative (ACR) Role Playing [audio CD]

Catapult your agency to growth — hire an ACR to keep the chair in front of your desk full of interested prospects every day. This lively and entertaining CD takes you through setting ACR goals right through to a whole host of scripts that are guaranteed to get appointments. This is a "must have" CD for agencies of every size.

FOR MORE INFORMATION GO TO
WWW.TKSYSTEMS.ORG
OR CALL 1-800-524-6390

An executive workshop to develop a strategic
and tactical plan for agency growth.

# Unleash the Power of your Agency.